Marking the Gospel

Marking the Gospel

A Devotional Commentary on the Gospel of Mark

Jody Seymour

RESOURCE *Publications* · Eugene, Oregon

MARKING THE GOSPEL
A Devotional Commentary on the Gospel of Mark

Resource Publications
An Imprint of Wipf and Stock Publishers
199 W. 8th Ave., Suite 3
Eugene, OR 97401
www.wipfandstock.com

ISBN 13: 978-1-61097-340-3
Manufactured in the U.S.A.

To
my wife Betsy
who loves me even
in those times when
"I miss the mark"

And to
Gail Spach
who carefully "marked"
this manuscript with
her insightful editing.

Contents

Preface

SOME ANIMALS ARE KNOWN to "mark" their territory. "X marks the spot" is a familiar saying, even to a child. The Greek word for sin is "harmatia," which literally means "to miss the mark." In this book I want to share in a journey with you in which we explore what it means to "mark" the Gospel. I want the hero of Mark's Gospel to make a mark on you. I want for you to end up being a marked man or, to be inclusive, a marked person.

Each of us is marked by something. We bear the mark of parents who—hopefully—did the best they could, but who made the inevitable mistakes in attempting to shape a human being. We bear the imprints of a culture that seems to cry out to us that instant is better than long-lasting, entertainment is better than joy, now is better than later, fact is deeper than truth, and the material is better than the spiritual because it can be quantified.

Countering these messages from our culture are the Gospels and their call to a different way of life. The first book we know of that was written about the Christian way of marking life was a short bit of propaganda that we now call *The Gospel of Mark*. Most scholars believe it was the first Gospel written, and that it became the framework of the storyline for subsequent pieces of propaganda entitled *The Gospel of Matthew* and *The Gospel of Luke*.

Do not be upset by my use of the descriptive word "propaganda." It is meant to help you understand that Mark and the other Gospels are not straightforward biographies of a famous man. The differences in the Gospel accounts are, in part, because each of the writers had a definite agenda to present, and a different audience on which they were trying to make their marks.

In modern-day terms, these Gospel accounts are loaded material. They do not pretend to be unbiased reporting. A slanted media is not a new phenomenon. Mark has a definite slant to his writing. What I want to do in this devotional commentary is to let that slant do its number on you. I want to let this slant make its mark on you, the reader.

The Gospel of Mark is meant to make an impression. It is not meant to be a general landscape in your life. It is meant to be a mark on the map. The power of Mark's Gospel can be missed because of its brevity. However, since it was the first mark made, I think we ought to pay close attention to its power to transform.

I call this work a devotional commentary because we will look carefully at the details of what Mark is saying, but for the purpose of letting it make an impression on us. Study will be in the background, not the foreground of this work. One of the teachers I had during the course of my undergraduate education, Dr. Walter P. Weaver, has written a commentary on Mark. His commentary on Mark in the *Basic Bible Commentary* series is part of the underpinning of this devotional commentary. I have also used Lamar Williamson Jr.'s commentary on Mark in the *Interpretation* series as background study for this devotional commentary.

If you desire the scholarship piece of this work, then purchasing those commentaries, or ones similar, will be of help to you. My desire in this book is to help you experience the meaning of the text for yourself.

It is my belief that the true inspiration of Scripture is not just in the writing of it, but also in the encounter with it. I believe that, in some way, God has chosen to have inspiration happen in the space between reader and writer. Modern science tells us that the perception of an event actually determines the nature of that event. Is light a particle or a wave? It depends on how you attempt to observe it. The observing actually affects the reality. Light is both particle and wave.

So it is with Scripture about the one who came to be known as the "light of the world." In Scripture a reality exists before we observe it, but something happens when we encounter its power. A cursory dealing with Scripture will miss its true reality. Spending time with the text and allowing it to mark you—that is the power of the inspired word of God.

So come with me on a journey of discovery. Pretend it is the first day of school and you are a child who has just bought that new pack of fresh paper. Remember the feeling of new beginnings. All things are possible. The pages are blank, ready for your impressions as you encounter new knowledge.

Could this earliest story of Jesus do that again for you? Can you perhaps feel the excitement of those who first hear the words: "The beginning of the gospel—the good news—of Jesus Christ, the Son of God"? Come with me and let us mark the Gospel. In so doing, I believe we will ourselves be marked.

Introduction

The Book of Mark

EVERY FAMILY HAS STORIES that are told over and over again. At family gatherings or reunions, the stories are pulled out and retold by an ever-aging community. Some of the newer additions to the clan hear the stories for the first time. Others hear them and start smiling even before the end comes.

These veterans are so familiar with the events that are being described, or at least with the telling of them, that they could relate the story themselves. Each one could tell it in their own way; different memories would come to the surface, different details. Each story would be colored by perspective.

Like an old oil painting, each time the story is told another layer of texture and color is added by the artist of the day. After years of painting, the canvas is both rich with color and layered not only with tradition but with the accumulation of the artists' interpretations.

The book we now call *The Gospel of Mark* is such a painting. Scholars have examined the pigments in detail. After careful examination, these scholars tell us that this particular canvas seems to be the oldest of the four canvases we call the four Gospels. When Matthew and Luke wrote their Gospels, they seem to have actually had access to the canvas that was Mark's Gospel. They used it as a model and added their own mixture of oils.

Modern biblical scholarship sometimes gets so focused on trying to determine each of the color pigments and their layered effect, and the big picture gets so separated into its elements, that the story the picture originally tried to tell becomes lost in the details. A sentence from one of Shakespeare's sonnets can be diagrammed on a piece of paper. The forms of grammar and sentence structure become clear, but the beauty and deep meaning of the poem fades.

This does not mean that the sacred text should not be seen for its layered reality. Not to do so ignores the way the Bible is written and edited. I have studied this writing and editing and find it fascinating and full of marvelous findings. It is appropriate to study the details that make up the texture of the canvas because not to do so can sometimes lead to rigid statements which begin "The Bible says. . . ." Such lack of study can lead to misunderstandings and may also result in the loss of much of the beauty and deep meaning of the Bible.

I want for us to get close enough to the Gospel of Mark to see that it is a layered canvas, but I do not want to lose the wonderful flavor of the family reunion story. Sure, my telling of family stories may be different from my grandmother's telling of the same stories, but the meaning and reason for telling them are the same.

Mark's family first put brush to canvas around 70 AD. The benchmark for this dating is the destruction of the Temple in Jerusalem. This event made the same impact on the Jewish/Christian community back then as would the destruction of the Capitol building in Washington, DC, in our time.

Some of the brush strokes on the canvas reflect this particular time in history and the pigments themselves do not seem to be much older than 70 AD. This means that the story had been told at family gatherings for around thirty years before someone decided to actually put oil to canvas. The Gospel of Mark is not then a portrait of Jesus painted by someone who was there making sketches during his lifetime. There are too many details left out for that to be true.

The edition of the Gospel of Mark that we have is the picture painted by the family telling the story as they had been hearing it for over thirty years. It is not the original painting but the end result of many layers of colors that had been blended together over the years. That is just the way it is.

Chapter One

"THE BEGINNING OF THE GOSPEL OF JESUS CHRIST, THE SON OF GOD."

Tradition has it that the first two Europeans who rode their horses through the forest and appeared on the other side of it to view the Grand Canyon for the first time said one to another, "Something happened here!" The power of understatement is evident in such a small sentence. Billions of years' worth of nature's power was wrapped up in a few words from two men who stood looking into a history that dwarfed their tiny existence.

Such is the case as Mark opens his book with a brief sentence that speaks volumes. The word "gospel" means "message about good news." This sentence is Mark's neon sign which flashes on and off throughout the entire book. Mark does not pretend that this book is a court stenographer's rendition of what has happened to a man who is a noble hero; Mark's story is going to be told more like that of an excited child, all out of breath, who has just come from seeing something that she wants others to witness. This opening sentence chimes out the purpose of the book much like the booming voice that comes over the speakers in a movie theater, and which causes everyone to sit up and take notice.

This is not to be the story of Jesus bar Joseph, the boy who grows up in Nazareth. This story is to be much more. This is the story to mark all of time. This is the story of one Jesus who is the Christ.

Today we say the phrase "Jesus Christ" as if Christ is his last name. The name has become too familiar. But this is no family name. This is a title which is to name a family. Christians are to be the ones who claim this name as their own because they are claimed by the one who is foretold by the prophets. This man is the one, the anointed one. He is not only the Jewish Messiah, which means he is the culmination of God's plan, but he is *the* Son of God. If you do not think this is jaw-dropping, stop now, because you are going to read the rest of the book too fast.

If I were to tell you that there is an asteroid the size of Texas coming toward Earth on a collision course, would you simply finish your cup of coffee and say, "Really?" and then go merrily off to work? This opening sentence in Mark's Gospel is meant to get your attention. This is the out-of-breath child telling you that the sky is falling, come look! This is the news that will make all news different.

This is *the* Son of God. Now before you get on your horse and ride off, remember that in Mark's Gospel there is no stable, no virgin birth, no wise men, no star, no angel voices announcing the first silent night. That is later and that's another story, or at least a different version of the story. The message of Mark is no Nicene Creed arguing the details of how it is that Jesus is the Son of God; Mark's opening words are an announcement that this man, whose birth is not even mentioned in this first gospel, is *the Son of God*.

Can you somehow remember how you first felt when you were told that Jesus was the Son of God? Probably not. You can bet that when Mark pens these words, a lot of people have not yet put two and two together. Mark is doing the math for them. Not only is Jesus the long-awaited Jewish deliverer, he is everybody's deliverer. God not only purchases a full page ad in the Jewish version of *USA Today*, via the Gospel of Mark, God buys time on *CNN* to tell the whole world that *the* son has arrived. This is news.

In Mark's Gospel Jesus never refers to himself as God's son. He waits for others to figure it out. God, of course, can't hold it in, so at Jesus' baptism, God jumps out of the cake and yells, "This is my boy! Wow, am I proud!"

But I'm getting ahead of myself. We all need to slow down.

The rest of Mark's Gospel is an unpacking of what the first sentence states. All the miracles, the demon exorcisms, the teaching and preaching, and the need to tell about why Jesus has to die, all are for the purpose of proving the first sentence.

MARK 1:2-8
JOHN OF THE DESERT

Anticipation is half of the joy of a long-awaited event. The aromas of cooking that emanate from the kitchen throughout Thanksgiving morning make the turkey and that favorite casserole all the more flavorful. Much of the joy of what has become of Christmas is looking at that wrapped package under the tree and trying to figure out what it is.

John of the desert is the wrapping on the package. He is not the package. Studies reveal that some people in that day think he is the package. They are anticipating the coming of someone who will get them out of the mess they are in. John fits the picture for many who come to hear him. Extreme times call for extreme measures, and John's hollering ways appeal to a people who are hungry for some word from God.

The silence of God has been deep and severe. The people figure that the dilemma they are in is of their own doing, and they are looking for some way to relieve their sense of guilt and change the course of their fortunes. The hated Romans and the sterile leaders of their faith make for a desert of belief. It is not easy for the common folks to get to the Temple in Jerusalem on the one hand, nor to pay their taxes to Rome on the other.

When John makes an appearance, he is neither wearing the robes of the scribes and the elders, nor is he exacting money. In his camel hair and leather girdle, he is asking for more than money. He demands repentance from everyone—including the guys wearing the robes—and he offers a water baptism for those who are seeking forgiveness.

John's way is the way of emptying and self-denial. He practices asceticism as a spiritual discipline. It is one of the ways we may prepare a way in our lives for God. There are times that we need this form of spirituality, especially when our lives become too cluttered and full. This cluttering may even take the shape of the amassing of religious "stuff." Religion can get in the way as much as it can help if religion becomes the ends rather than the means.

Water baptism is nothing new. The way John does it has flair and sure gets people's attention, but other groups perform water baptisms as a sign of initiation into their community. The idea of water cleansing someone is not novel. The reality that John's proclamation has the effect of drawing crowds of people out from the whole Judean countryside says more about the people's hunger and anticipation than about John's technique. The people are ready and waiting.

In that day, there is a common belief that Elijah will precede the coming of the Messiah. There is to be a warm-up band before the concert begins. Mark, through his description of John, identifies John with Elijah (see 2 Kings 1:8). John is the one-man-warm-up band.

Many people are so captivated by his performance, however, that he has to make it clear that he is simply getting the crowd ready for the main act. His closing number is a first-century way of saying, "You ain't seen nothing yet!" He speaks of his baptism being the rain that comes before the lightning. What he offers is water. The one who is to follow him will light up the sky with fire.

"The one who is more powerful than I is coming after me; I am not worthy to stoop down and untie the thong of his sandals. I have baptized you with water but he will baptize you with the Holy Spirit." (Mark 1:7–8). (What the Holy Spirit meant to those people in John's audience is anybody's guess.)

In Mark's Gospel the tension between the baptism of water and the baptism of the Holy Spirit is left to the imagination. Here is a reason to study more than one of the Gospel accounts in order to obtain the whole picture.

In the other Gospels (see Matthew 3:11–12, or Luke 3:15–17, for example), John the Baptist specifies that this baptism of fire will be harsh, "If you think I am a hell and brimstone preacher, you just wait till he gets here." John's spirituality was a desert way of spirituality. John may have been thinking that what the Messiah would bring would be a higher volume version of this desert spirituality.

Mark says nothing of this anticipation by John. Mark keeps it simple. From reading further in the Gospel of Mark, we can see that for Mark, Jesus comes to fill life with abundance. What we have between the lines in Mark's version of the story is a very different kind of spirituality from that of John's asceticism. Mark's Jesus goes to dinner parties and weddings. He speaks words about the flowers in the fields, and mustard seeds that grow into the greatest of shrubs, and does not say so much about the barrenness of the desert.

Water baptism, with its symbolic suggestion of death and new life, may be a sign of cleansing and of forgiveness by God, but it also has the ringing words of crusty old desert John as he reminds us of the letting go and emptying that is sometimes necessary for us to un-clutter the way to God. John's view by choice and design is narrow. The desert sun will do that to a prophet.

We do need the desert way of spirituality at times. The emptying effect is good for balance, but in the Gospel of Mark, the focus is on Jesus' understanding of a spirituality that is characterized by his words in the Gospel of John: "I came that they may have life, and have it abundantly." (John 10:10)

The baptism of the Holy Spirit is more expansive than some today would have it. The baptism of the Holy Spirit as practiced by Jesus is a baptism of fire, a fire of cleansing, and grants the person baptized the freedom to live abundantly and live out of a sense of sufficiency rather than scarcity. This is the reason that when someone is baptized in the Christian community all those who look on should hear the words, "Remember your baptism and be grateful."

MARK 1:9-11
THE BAPTISM OF JESUS

John's skin may be parched from the sun in the desert, but now he faces the Son in the desert. This is Mark's "birth story." The Son of God is "born" in the midst of the burning heat of the sun in the desert.

Mark has no soft angel's voice telling a wide-eyed Mary that a son is coming. There is no sweet story of a babe born in a manger. The Son of God is "birthed" in the blistering heat of repentance. How Jesus comes from the womb is of no concern to Mark. Arguments about a virgin birth are washed away in the waters of the Jordan.

Jesus comes out of the waters and hears a proud father say, "This is my beloved son in whom I am well pleased." And that's it. What happens before is left a mystery in Mark's story. All that matters is that from that moment on this young man is now the Son of God as announced by none other than God.

There is no mention of anyone other than Jesus hearing this announcement from the clouds. While in the other Gospels the event seems to be a public disclosure, this earliest Gospel seems to imply that this is between God and his boy. This theme of keeping things quiet is woven all through the gospel of Mark. Jesus' insistence oftentimes that people not reveal his identity is one of Mark's trademarks. Scholars call this theme the "messianic secret" motif.

I will not go into all the speculations as to why Mark does this. Not having angel choirs announcing the birth, and foreign "kings" coming from distant countries, fits in with the more subtle nature of Mark's Jesus.

One could ask if Mark knows of the manger tradition or the Magi tradition and chooses not to use them. The question goes unanswered for sure, although knowing about such occurrences and choosing not to use them seems to modern observers rather beyond imagining. Mark's depiction of Jesus reflects a figure who is not explicit in advertising who he is.

Even though the writings of Mark were used by Matthew and Luke, who both have birth traditions in their accounts of Jesus, we must allow the Gospel of Mark to stand on its own. That is hard to do for people who have grown up watching bath-robed shepherds, plastic babies in mangers, and tin-foil-crowned kings. We throw the various elements of the story together and blend them like making slaw out of cabbage. That may be fine for a local church Christmas pageant, but it takes away from the unique telling of the story by Mark.

For Mark, the only birth worth telling about is the one that happens to the Son in the desert sun that day of his baptism. The story begins privately and will continue to be private until Jesus decides to go public.

MARK 1:12-13
THE TEMPTATION OF JESUS

In Matthew and Luke the temptation story is a full-fledged drama. In Mark it is a couple of sentences. Mark leaves the listener asking, "What really happened out there in the wilderness?"

Mark's version of the temptation of Jesus is a reminder of the loneliness of the true struggle of temptation. We are left alone with our thoughts of what it must be like to be in the wilderness with only the wild beasts and Satan.

This abrupt account which follows the glory of Jesus' baptism is similar to the story of the young college football star who wins all sorts of honors and acclaim but who suddenly finds himself in training camp at the professional level. Being drafted number one by a team means having to prove oneself in the wilderness of training camp with the "wild beasts." It may also be a lot like what it would be like to be enrolled in a boot camp. Jesus has to test his ability to withstand what is coming in the days ahead.

The text says that the Spirit "drove" him out into the wilderness. This is not a choice. The only choice Jesus has is to decline the draft. Once Jesus accepts that he is the Son, he has to face the test. I wonder what would happen if this were the pattern for those who joined up to be Christian. Rather than receiving a new member packet and a copy of the church directory, new recruits to the church would be sent to training camp.

Could it be that today we do not believe, as did Mark, that what is involved in being a member of the Christian church is a cosmic struggle between the powers of evil and the powers of God? People who sign up as Christians today seem not to listen to the baptismal vows that are spoken in church which ask, "Do you renounce the spiritual forces of wickedness, and reject the evil powers of this world?"

The words are straightforward and clear, but we domesticate them. We tame the wild beasts and reduce Satan to a Halloween costume. In so doing we lose the reality that we are in a battle. The beasts seem tame but in fact sneak up on us in the guise of the lure to be less than who we are by trying to be more than who we are.

Jesus is driven into the wilderness because his Father knows he has to deal with the reality of what he is going to face the rest of his short-lived life. This is to be Jesus' boot camp. It is an interesting theological point that God figures that Jesus needs this testing. Jesus is not yet equipped to battle the powers of wickedness. He must first experience boot camp.

If Jesus needs to be equipped, I wonder if we need preparation in order to get ready for the work of discipleship. What would our boot camp need to look like in order to make us ready?

Notice that God does not do the tempting. That is Satan's role. Still is. Wouldn't it be great if Satan really was in a Halloween costume? Now the rascal has gone underground and reaches up from within to lead us in all sorts of directions. In the wilderness Satan can be seen for who Satan is: that which opposes God and good. Satan no longer needs the costume. The wilderness is always just around the corner.

Jesus does push-ups in the wilderness with Satan standing over in the shade offering him lemonade and attempting to persuade Jesus that all this conditioning work is not needed. Matthew and Luke, in their Gospel accounts, set up the lemonade stand for all the world to see. Mark has the reader fill in what the temptations might look like.

Angels are in the wilderness too. As with the temptations, Mark does not put wings on the angels. For Mark, angels are simply God's way of getting to Jesus while not preventing him from doing his needed conditioning. The angels offer Jesus lemonade too, but only after he finishes the push-ups. You can bet Jesus has a time of it in the wilderness not only deciding which voices to listen to but when to listen to them. We have the same problem.

Satan and God can sometimes offer us the same thing. Timing is important. Grace is sometimes best utilized after the work is done, especially if the work is the necessary work one has to do on the interior life.

At other times, what God offers and what Satan offers are quite different. The choice is clear, but the problem comes when we have not done our necessary push-ups and therefore find ourselves not being able to resist Satan using only our own strength.

Angels are still available if called upon. Do not expect angels to be winged creatures any more than you can expect demons to be pitch-forked, but angels are listening. God knows how lonely the wilderness can get. If Jesus needed help out there, I suppose we do too.

MARK 1:14–15
JESUS' MESSAGE

Mark does not waste words. Perhaps Mark is not the favorite Gospel for preachers. We preachers tend to use a lot of words to get our points across. However, most of us are told in seminary that we need to express the main idea of our sermons in one sentence.

Mark knows how to be succinct. He uses one sentence to set the place, and another to state the main idea. John's business is done; it is time for the main attraction. For Mark nothing more needs to be said about John.

Other Gospel writers find themselves not able to get rid of crusty old John so easily, but for Mark, John's role is simply to set the stage and step off. Mark then places Jesus in Galilee where he will spend the next eight chapters. Jesus' role, according to Mark, is to "proclaim the good news of God." Here we have a concise phrase which says it all but which can mean many different things.

In the movie *City Slickers,* a city slicker on vacation is playing at being a cowboy. He and a few friends pay big bucks to be with some real cowboys in a cattle drive. Sitting uncomfortably on a horse, the city slicker looks up into the eyes of Curly, a rugged cowboy of few words who acts as if he just couldn't care less about these cowboy wannabes from the city.

Curly looks down from his horse into the eyes of the city boy and asks, "You know what the secret of life is?"

"No, what is it?" the intimidated wannabe replies.

Curly raises his leather-glove-covered hand and points to the sky with one finger. Then he gazes at his solitary raised finger and drawls, "It's *this*."

Curious, the city slicker questions," And what *is* that?"

With an enigmatic smile, Curly responds, "That is what *you* have to find out."

Jesus raises his index finger in the air and tells us that the secret of life is *this*, the good news of the kingdom of God. And what is this good news about the kingdom of God? Jesus now invites us, "Come and let's find out."

Part of the good news is about the timing. It seems that whatever *this* is, it has "come near," it is "at hand." What people in Mark's Gospel will discover is that the reason *this* is at hand is that *he* has come near. Jesus is the dawning of something entirely new.

The good news is that the secret is revealed. The not-so-good news to many who will listen to this secret of the meaning of life is that they are going to have to turn around from their old ways. The word Jesus uses is "repent."

Part of the secret of life was, and is, to turn around, take a look, and go in a different direction. To stay on the same old, tired course is not what Jesus comes to offer. The kingdom of God has something to do with change and new beginnings. Many will find out that this change is not a matter of a slight alteration but rather a radical change in direction.

This is not going to be a matter of putting a new roof over an old roof. This repentance means tearing off the old roof and first letting the light in. Then comes the new roof. All through Mark's Gospel Jesus will keep that one finger raised. People will ask what the raised finger means and Jesus will tell them. Some people will start tearing off shingles, other people will try simply to put a new roof over an old one, and many more people will decide that their old roof is fine, "thank you very much!"

MARK 1:16–20
CALLING THE FIRST DISCIPLES

Do you remember the first time you fell in love? The words in such a phrase are well used because it is usually indeed a falling. And falling in love can be a glorious thing. But what happens when you get up again after falling? Of course no one dares asks such a question. Falling in love is not supposed to be rational. Falling in love is falling into passion. To be blind to reason is part of the fun of falling in love.

Life is full of hard decisions and unexpected tragedy. Falling in love is one of the best parts of the script of life that we do not write. I hope you have been able to fall in love at least once, even if there was pain involved later on—and there usually is.

If you understand falling in love, or understand it as much as any human can, you can remotely understand how the first disciples simply leave everything to follow Jesus. It is a passionate decision. You can bet that Zebedee, the father of James and John, sure tries to knock some reason into his two headstrong, in-love sons. He needs those boys to help run the fishing business and here they are jumping out of the boat and into another life.

Zebedee overhears Jesus saying that he will make his boys "fishers of men." This frightened father probably says something like, "Well that's fine, Jesus, but who is going to catch the regular old fish that my family depends on to make a living?"

Falling in love is not about reason. In the other Gospel accounts there may be a hint that the sudden leaving behind of everything by certain disciples necessitates that they already know about Jesus and who he is. Mark's Gospel is more like a love story in which these disciples are simply swept off their feet by this new man's preaching about a coming kingdom that is going to change everything.

Peter, Andrew, James, and John are like slaphappy boys who hear the marching band calling new recruits to the glories of fighting for a noble cause. All they hear is the music. They do not hear the distant sounds of guns. Scenes of wounded comrades and lonely nights away from home are drowned out by the sound of joyous music.

"Follow me, now, this instant, and I will have you catching people." The song sounds too good to pass up. Maybe fishing has grown too ordinary for these full-blooded men. Jesus sees something in their eyes that is worth fishing for—and Jesus is quite a fisherman. He has these young boys hooked before they know what is happening.

He does not bother to tell them that day about a cross. At this moment he wants their enthusiasm. They will need that zeal. Jesus will need that zeal, though he often does not get it from his small band of disciples. The first smell of the battle softens these boys real quick, but the tales of softening come later.

For now, the scene is of an old man standing in a boat shaking his head as his boys and two of their friends walk into the sunset and away from the boats. "What fools they are," this father thinks ruefully. He is right.

Chapter Two

MARK 2:1–12
JESUS HEALS THE PARALYTIC IN CAPERNAUM

In compiling his Gospel, Mark puts a number of traditions together. What we have in Mark is a mosaic. He uses different tiles to create his mosaic. These tiles come from various sources that Mark has in his possession. Biblical scholars would lick their chops to be able to look over Mark's shoulder as he puts together his mosaic.

If Mark has different buckets of tiles, which bucket does he pick from in order to place Jesus "at home" in Capernaum, as he is said to be in this account? Everybody knows that Jesus' home is Nazareth, right? Maybe one of Mark's buckets has Jesus' home located in Capernaum. In Mark's telling of the story, Jesus does seem to spend a lot of time in Capernaum. Does Jesus' family move to Capernaum later? Tradition has it that Joseph dies while Jesus is young. It is possible that Mary moves to Capernaum to be with or near relatives. Go ahead, reach into your own bucket and imagine.

One never knows how much weight to put on one piece of tile. It may be that Mark simply puts in a tile that he is given, or that he is making a theological statement. It is important to remember that the Bible is a rich mosaic and not a simple paint-by-number, one-dimensional picture. We must honor the nature of how our Scriptures are put together. Since no one is looking over Mark's shoulder, there will be different opinions as to what Mark is doing as he tells the Jesus story.

Theologically speaking, maybe we are not to know where Jesus' home is. Jesus' home is where the works of God happen. Jesus is at home where people believe in the Son of Man.

Whatever *home* means, and to get back to the story, Jesus is there when four people show up carrying a paralyzed man. The four men cannot get near Jesus because of the crowd that has gathered. Mark has already made Jesus a star by the end of chapter one, with his brief mention of how Jesus' fame is now established throughout all of Galilee. Remember, he is telling the Jesus story with a sense of urgency.

Mark simply states, "It was reported that he was at home," and that is all it takes for a crowd to gather. One can imagine the scene of people packed into the tiny dwelling. Jesus does not hang out with wealthy people nor does he come from rich stock. Home is a one room, hut-like dwelling with a thatched roof. Stairs are placed on one side of the small house for perhaps climbing onto the roof to catch the cool evening breezes. Air-conditioning is a few centuries away, and creativity is the order of the day when it comes to getting cool.

Mark wants us to really see this scene. The clue to this is that he takes so many verses to describe the picture. Mark has evidently put two scenes together. Those who study such things tell us that Mark takes a healing story and puts it with another theme that he wants to portray, that of Jesus' forgiveness of sins.

Healing stories usually take the form of a description of the person to be healed, an action by the healer, a pronouncement of the healing, and a proclamation by the person healed. Mark inserts into this standard formula the added element of the forgiveness of sins. Even the original language betrays an interruption in the text. Mark puts in another tile in order to tell his story. Mark knows that it is the fact that Jesus is going around forgiving sins that gets him into real trouble with the scribes and authorities. Mark wants to get this into his story early.

For those of us in the present day who read Mark's words, his mosaic creates questions. Does sin cause illness? In Jesus' day many people believe that it does. The old Deuteronomic ethic teaches that if something is physically wrong with you, either you or your parents must have committed a terrible sin. Jesus appears to be participating in this ethic.

Stepping back from the mosaic pieces and seeing the total picture allows us to see that while Jesus probably does understand the intricate relationship between psychological health and physical well-being, he definitely does not believe in the causal relationship of sin and sickness that his peers share.

The scribes, conveniently, are present in this crowded scene. It is crowded literally and theologically. The scribes do not get that Jesus is bringing in a new kingdom in which sins are forgiven by the Son of Man. All the scribes can think about is that their old kingdom has no room in it for some upstart to be forgiving sins.

Jesus "perceives in his spirit" that the scribes are questioning his actions and asks them if it is easier to say, "Get up and walk, you are well," or, "Your sins are forgiven." Jesus is a good reader of faces. He does not even have to wait for the scribes to raise their hands at this first-century press conference. Jesus notices their whispers and their looks of disbelief as he deals with this bound-up man struggling with paralysis.

Jesus perceives a lot of things. He knows what the scribes are thinking, and he knows that sin did not cause this man's legs to be paralyzed. He may also know that the man on the pallet likely believes that sin is his captor. Remember, Jesus is dealing with people who are living around him at that time. We sometimes think that Jesus is talking only to us—"Jesus loves me this I know, for the Bible tells me so."—True, but Jesus loved the people in the Bible first. We often forget to honor who they are. Probably this man believes that his sin or his parent's sin caused his illness. Jesus here frees him from both the bindings of his erroneous past beliefs and the physical bondage of paralysis.

Jesus has the ability to deal with whatever comes up. The poor old scribes are one-dimensional in their view. They simply cannot handle this man whose difficulties are both physical and spiritual. That is part of the scribes' problem. The scribes have made religion one-dimensional and empty. The people are, as one song puts it, "standing knee deep in a river and dying of thirst." Jesus comes to give people some much-needed water. He does it by opening up the gap between the physical and the spiritual world and showing the relationship between the two.

Mark puts these two worlds together in this one story. Jesus' whole life is a story of helping people see the relationship between the physical and the spiritual, but after all, papyrus is a rare commodity and Mark has only so much time. Mark puts a number of elements together; those of us who read his words can step back and look at the total picture.

Jesus calls himself "Son of Man" here for the first time. The people of Jesus' day hear this as a reference to the triumphant apocalyptic figure in Daniel to whom was given "dominion, glory and kingship."(See Daniel 7: 13–14). Jesus evidently wants people's ears to perk up when he uses this title. He wants them to know that for sure that something big is happening.

Jesus later turns this apocalyptic image on its head by the way he lives out the role. Many people do not like this change. The people in Jesus day are weary of waiting for deliverance. They want an angel-like, conquering figure to come in and vaporize the Romans, use a magic wand to alter the hearts of the religious leaders, and cut Caesar's throat. This *Son of Man* fails on all counts.

Jesus is at home in Capernaum because he forgives sins and releases a man from the bondage of infirmity. Home is where the heart is and Jesus' heart is wrapped around forgiving sins and freeing people for a new life. The scribes cannot see the forest for the trees nor can they see the big picture for the tiles. All they can see is a popular upstart who does not have the proper credentials to be messing with the forgiveness of sins.

Forgiving sins is a monopoly, and the established religion as it is practiced at that time, with its specific Temple rituals and sacrifices, has a market on the product. The Temple is rather like the old U.S. telephone system, *Ma Bell*. It does not want the break-up of what it considers to be a good thing.

Jesus is not interested in monopolies and knows that it is time for a change. Mark's telling of the story is built around a threatened break-up of the religious monopoly. The solution to keeping the monopoly in place is handled in a late night negotiation resulting in a crucifixion. The seeds for a "final solution" are planted in this chapter.

The first twelve verses of Mark chapter two can be seen as a parallel of the entire Gospel of Mark: A new kingdom is being initiated that will not be tolerated by the old kingdom. Mark knows the end of the story and wants the reader to already begin seeing the handwriting on the wall.

On one level, the healing of the man affected by paralysis can be understood as an allegory. Sin binds us. Faith can free us from our bindings. We can walk into a new life if we believe. Does this mean that the story does not literally happen?

If I see a butterfly and tell a child that the butterfly is like resurrection, it does not mean the butterfly is not a butterfly. Jesus heals a man who is brought to him by people who believe that Jesus has power to set people free. Their efforts are rewarded by a healing story that we now have forever. Jesus heals the man's legs and then frees his soul from the burden of the heavy chains of shame. He does the latter at no extra charge since the first liberation is also free. Unlike the professional scribes who murmur to themselves about this release, Jesus does not charge for his services of forgiveness.

You can leave your turtle doves and money at home. They are marketable in the old kingdom but their value is undermined in the new kingdom that Jesus brings. Freedom is in the air, and it is dangerous.

MARK 2:13-17
THE CALL OF LEVI/EATING WITH TAX COLLECTORS

I love Mark's geography. It is both picturesque and theological. Here we find Jesus "out again beside the sea," with "the whole crowd gathered around him." I have been privileged to walk beside this sea. I experienced why Jesus must have loved it so. His life was so crowded and this sea is so inviting and expansive.

I imagine Jesus rising early before his disciples and simply looking out over this sea. In actuality it is a lake compared to many of the seas on our planet. But to the people of Jesus' day, and to Jesus I imagine, it is indeed a sea of possibilities. Out of it comes industry. Out if it come a good number of Jesus' disciples. He plucks Peter, James, John and Andrew from their nets with remnants of this sea still dripping from the webbing.

It is beside this sea that Mark places Jesus for a series of controversy stories. One must remember that, as Mark shared these stories, his audience was involved in their own set of controversies. Mark's audience was the early church. They were embroiled in arguments over who might sit at the table with them, and who was allowed inside the community of believers. There were very definite standards of who was *in* and who was *out*. Against such a backdrop, Mark retold the stories of chapter two.

Levi is unknown after this story. He is not mentioned again. Early tradition equates him with Matthew the tax collector, but no such connection is made by Mark. Levi is simply a tax collector who has his table set up somewhere by the sea. This is rather like a first-century lemonade stand, except that the lemonade on offer to the people is really more just a bitter taste in their mouths—but they have to pay the price anyway.

The tax collectors are hated by the people and by the Jewish establishment. Tax collectors are usually Jewish locals who are under contract by the government. They siphon off some money for themselves when they collect the taxes, and siphon it off again before they pay their Roman bosses.

Who knows why Levi responds so quickly to Jesus' request to "follow me"? Mark is a master at leaving it to the imagination. Can it be that Levi simply follows out of curiosity? Maybe he is tired of his way of making it. Is Levi so surprised that someone like Jesus makes such an offer that Levi simply goes along for the ride? Or is Levi, like others whom Jesus encounters, just ripe for the picking? Perhaps one of Jesus' divine attributes is a kind of radar that can target those who are ready, as in the familiar saying, "When you are ready to learn the teacher will come."

Mark uses this story of Levi to make a point. Jesus ends up in Levi's house. The place is as full of sinners as a barroom is full of smoke. If you have ever been in such a barroom, and are not a smoker, then you remember that when you come out, you reek of smoke. If you get this picture, you will understand what the scribes of the Pharisees say next.

According to them, because Jesus lowers himself to eat with tax collectors and those sinners who do not keep the Jewish law, Jesus reeks with the smell of the company he keeps. He renders himself "unclean."

The law-abiding scribes of the Pharisees point this out to Jesus. Jesus waves his hand just enough to clear the smoke from in front of his face and informs the non-smoking clergy that those who do not need to quit smoking are unlikely to need a patch. (For those of you who have lost my imagery, a nicotine patch is a smoking cessation aid. This is a good example of the maxim that if you have to explain an image it begins to lose something. This is why Mark does so little explaining in his gospel.)

Jesus responds to the scribes that "those who are well have no need of a physician." Jesus is making it clear that he has come for people who are aware that they need help. Jesus also breaks the crystal vase that the religious establishment has been keeping on the shelf. The crystal container is meant to hold something very precious, but it has become a museum piece whose main purpose is to collect the dust of the ages.

Jesus breaks the container like the glass that is broken at a Jewish wedding. He announces to the keepers of the crystal that fine crystal is *out* and the cheap glass is *in*. He wants to offer water to the thirsty and he knows that the folks by the sea will not drink anything from crystal containers.

Jesus may as well have kicked in the door to Levi's house and let everybody in. Jesus loves to kick in doors. When he kicks in the door on this particular night, smoke comes pouring out. After all, to continue with the smoking analogy, these are smokers. What did the Pharisees expect to see?

Although Jesus does not smoke, he smells like smoke his whole ministry. He never lights up but he still loves the people who do. Jesus ends up hanging out with them a lot, and many of them end up kicking the habit. Jesus has a keen sense of smell. He can smell the smoke on the

Pharisees' robes even when others cannot. He guesses that they are the kind who preach sermons about the evils of smoking only to light up late at night when no one is looking. Needless to say, the Pharisees do not like anyone blowing their cover or smelling their clothes.

The Pharisees either have to find another way to wash out their clothes and hang them out to dry so that the smoke will clear, or they have to find a way to hang Jesus out to dry. Guess which plan is on their minds?

MARK 2:18-28
CONTROVERSY OVER THE OLD AND THE NEW

Giving up things has a long tradition in religious practice. Fasting is like a Hallmark greeting card when it comes to piety. Fasting shows "you really care." The religious leaders of Jesus' day love to send greeting cards. Too often, however, they like to flaunt their faith by wearing T-shirts with slogans. John's disciples evidently wear T-shirts that say "Fasting R Us." Fasting is one of their defining traditions.

It seems that John's disciples are lean and mean in their style. Some of them think the end is right around the corner and they want to be found ready by not being engulfed by the world. They fast regularly to be like first-century Boy Scouts; on the back of the T-shirts reads a complementary phrase, "Be Prepared."

While Jesus acknowledges that there is value to the spiritual discipline of fasting, and that there are appropriate times for fasting, he does not so much appreciate the way they have of drawing attention to their devotion. Outward signs are important to them, but Jesus is more interested in the inward sources of their devotion.

Let us not misunderstand Jesus here. There is the danger of making him into yet another slogan, like the line from Forrest Gump, "Life is like a box of chocolates. You never know what you're gonna get." Jesus affirms the practice of fasting, but declares that now is neither the time, nor the place for it.

Jesus takes a bite out of the way of viewing things of his contemporaries. They are concerned with outward signs of devotion and being prepared for the end, but Jesus asks, "Why fast when the party is going on?" He announces to the fasting groups of his day that "the time is at hand," the bridegroom is present. This is not the time for fasting. Mark's emphasis in these verses is on the joy and the abundance of life that Jesus is offering.

Change is hard for religious types. We get stuck easily within our comfort zones. In the next few verses of this chapter in Mark, Jesus speaks of how things need to change because old ways can sometimes be like oil that has not been changed in an engine. Things get sluggish and it is not at all good for the overall running of the engine.

Since the engine analogy does not quite fit (we are a long time from Henry Ford after all), Jesus uses what is at hand and understandable to his audience. He speaks of sewing an un-shrunk piece of new fabric onto an old garment. Jesus also uses the image of putting new wine in old wineskins. Both practices result in ripping or spilling.

Jesus is getting his audience ready for some ripping and spilling. The theological irony is that these two verbs describe what end up happening to Jesus. The old is not ready for the new. Trying to sew a Jesus patch onto existing fabric still has its problems. Jesus is speaking of the need for a whole new garment.

Can it be that what is happening in our present day is that many people want simply to sew a Jesus patch onto their daily outfits and go on about business as usual? When the laundry is done, the wearer may discover that the new patch has pulled away from the old garment.

Mark then tells a story to make Jesus' point. This would be like the preacher on Sunday morning stopping the sermon and pointing to a chancel drama for emphasis. Actions, especially dramatic ones, speak louder than words.

Jesus' disciples are caught eating grain from a field on the Sabbath. The Jews considered the Sabbath, one of their oldest traditions, not to be tampered with. However, not only do Jesus' disciples *not* tip-toe carefully through the tulips, they trample all over everything. This field is not filled with tulips but with grain. They eat the grain because they are in need.

The Pharisees, like children watching other children do something wrong, tattle on the law breakers. It is the Sabbath. To break it in this way is an ultimate no-no. In the story, Jesus drops a few lines of Scripture about how *the* hero of the faith, David himself, had him some fast food one Sabbath.

Most commentators say that Jesus stretches the point here. The example that Jesus uses does not exactly fit. The disciples are eating grain from a field, while King David takes some of the specially consecrated bread from the temple. By doing this, Jesus helps all preachers out who reach deep to make an example fit the theme.

Jesus defends this use of an old story by stating that his general point is that something new has arrived, and the old way of seeing and doing will not fit.

Jesus finally just goes ahead and says what he means, "I am Lord of the Sabbath!" You can bet that got some people's attention. Some of the Pharisees can be heard in the back of the crowd saying something like, "Did he say he was bored with the Sabbath? What's the matter with him?"

When the correction is made, the crowd gets real quiet, and someone hears the sound of a garment being torn or wine being spilled all over the ground. The old is not going to handle the new. The religious establishment does not need or want a "Lord." There is but one Lord and they already have him boxed in the Temple. The religious leaders want no one, especially some upstart from Nazareth or Capernaum, or wherever he is from, messing with the old traditions.

"Lord of the Sabbath, really! Somebody needs to take him down a notch or two." Plans are heard in the background even in these early chapters of Mark. Mark wants to make it crystal clear just why Jesus is hung up to dry like some piece of cloth.

Jesus is more interested in human need than he is in religious practice. This was and is good news for humankind, but not such good news for the establishment. Institutional religion easily gains a self-preserving quality. Jesus was and is a constant challenge to those who think they have finally got the recipe for the best wine or who finish sewing the garment and want no new additions.

Jesus wants people fed no matter what day it is. He wants power to be present no matter how uncomfortable it makes those who like it the way it has always been. And yes, he will tear things up if need be to make sure that people stay alive to the constantly changing spirit which "blows where it wills." I know that is from another Gospel but it applies to the same Lord.

Chapter Three

HEALING THE MAN WITH A WITHERED HAND

"What makes Jesus mad?" would be a good title for this section. Those who want to make Jesus some kind of moral policeman who stands by with a set of the Ten Commandments and keeps score are disappointed with the findings in these verses. In these verses the very ones who anger Jesus are the ones who want him to be that moral policeman.

A good deal of religious practice is based on a God who is like Santa Claus—"making a list and checking it twice, gonna find out who's naughty or nice." Jesus is more concerned with the source of a person's actions. He keeps talking about matters of the heart, the heart being the seat of emotions and thought for the Jewish people.

Keeping the rules for the sake of keeping the rules is not enough, and it can lead to empty ritual and self-righteous merit badge collecting. Jesus has a way of seeing through actions and looking for attitudes. If it is a question of giving someone a cup of water, Jesus would be interested in where the water is drawn from. For Jesus, the reasons for actions reveal more than the actions themselves.

The people who make Jesus mad are the ones who forget the reason that God made guidelines in the first place. God is not concerned with list-keeping nor is God impressed by the quantity of rules that one keeps. God loves. God wants wholeness for God's people. God knows best, and God knows what hurts people. God knows that we are less than God, and we were supposed to be less than God. God set up parameters within which to operate. God does not box us in but allows us to be free.

Many of the Pharisees and other religious leaders of Jesus' day are box sellers. They get so busy making sure everyone has the right box that they forget what the box is supposed to hold. Goodness of life is for everyone. When Jesus asks, "Is it lawful to do good or to do harm on the Sabbath?" he is met with silence.

Jesus is aware that his listeners already know the answer. Jesus understands that those being asked to respond to his question have been boxed in. This boxing-in makes Jesus mad. Those who are uncomfortable with Jesus being mad will just have to get over it. The word that Mark used to describe Jesus' anger means "to be really disgusted." He is so disgusted that he grieves for those with whom he is angry.

If you have ever looked at someone who has made you angry and they are angry back at you and you say, "You know, I feel really sorry for you," then you get the picture. Jesus is saying to the religious leaders, "You don't get it, do you? You have forgotten the reason for the Sabbath. You have closed down your hearts. Your hearts are fossilized. They have grown old, hard, and without feeling. They represent death and not life."

If you have trouble believing that Jesus meant all this with the use of one phrase, then look it up in a good commentary. Mark's use of the Greek language, based on the idiom of Jesus' day, reveals a multi-layered meaning in many phrases. In other words they had some better ways of saying what something means than we do. One phrase could say many things.

Jesus is sick to his heart over the religious leadership of his father's house. Before he ever goes to Jerusalem, Jesus, by means of his words and deeds, symbolically turns over the tables in the synagogue. On the tables are all those boxes full of regulations that the religious leaders have used to hem in the people. Jesus wants the contents of those boxes out on the floor for all to see. The new has arrived. The old is going to have to be broken open in order to contain the new. The boxes are too small.

But boxes are an important product of the religious establishment. No wonder it is in this section that Mark reveals for the first time in explicit language that they start plotting how to get rid of him.

Lest we forget that there is a healing story in all this, let us remember the man with a withered hand. Mark seems more interested in the Pharisees' contempt for Jesus' perceived disrespect towards the Sabbath. The healing of the man with a withered hand seems secondary. To Mark, it is secondary. Mark assumes the healing ministry of Jesus and usually gives little detail about the healing itself.

The assumptions made by the writer of Mark's Gospel would make a book unto themselves. We might like to know more about the background assumptions of this first and oldest gospel, but Mark keeps us guessing. His writing almost assumes that the reader already buys into certain things about Jesus. Jesus is a healer. That is assumed.

Mark has no way of knowing the questions that would arise years later about some of his assumptions. How does Jesus heal? Why does he not heal everybody? Why does healing not happen more today like it did when Jesus touched people?

All of these are pretty good questions which Mark leaves unanswered. Jesus' healings are, in my book, pretty spectacular. But is this some kind of tease? I have personally not seen withered hands made whole with one touch of a human hand. Yes, I know there are miracles of modern surgery and medicine, but I am talking about those things that look like they happen on TV when some screaming voice beckons a person in a wheelchair to walk.

We have all seen the scenes on TV and anyone who wants to take the time to investigate will discover the emptiness of many of those "healings." Mind control, hysteria, and even set up fake healings are usually what are behind many of these spectacular episodes.

The Gospel of Mark clearly states that Jesus is the unique bearer of a new kingdom. As a sign of this kingdom, Jesus heals. Mark believes in the demons of his day. In our day and age, we can demythologize those demons, but to Mark they are demons. Jesus, as we shall see later in this chapter has the demons' number. A new power is breaking into the world. This is the power of the man from heaven.

For Jesus, to heal is not really a big deal. In the completion of this new kingdom there will be healing for everyone. What is soon discovered is that *our* kingdom cannot handle the completeness of this *new* kingdom. There are still healings that happen. We cannot box up those healings. There is mystery to healing, for there is a mystery to the way the kingdom of God touches our kingdom.

We can offer healing in the name of Jesus, but we are not Jesus. He is a one-time event. He is the bearer of a kingdom which is both here in part, and not yet. Jesus gives us a glimpse of the "not yet" in his healings. Jesus does, however, go away.

The power of his spirit is with us. Healing and wholeness can happen in the name of that Spirit, but it is not as patterned and controlled as many "healers" claim it to be. I have the same anger as Jesus had when I see the manipulation done in his name.

For Jesus, there is no mystery in healing. He simply does it. When we see him face to face we too shall receive the full benefit of that healing. In this life, where the kingdom of God struggles to be felt and made real, healing is not as evident.

I know there are miraculous, sudden healings that cannot be explained. They are few in terms of all that could be and all that are needed. I will not package the healing of God nor do I believe anyone can. Jesus is a pattern in many ways, but there can be some danger in those who think they can also say boldly, "Stretch out your hand." Some things are to be left to Jesus.

To pray for healing in the name of Jesus is most appropriate, but there is always an element of letting it be after the prayer is said. I fully believe that when I lay my hands on someone or anoint them with oil and ask for God's healing grace for their lives, that God gives a measure of healing to that person. I am not to control or package what kind of healing that will be.

Usually I do not get the kind of physical healing I desire when I pray such a healing prayer for someone. I have seen many cases of healing of relationships, emotional healing, and spiritual growth come from such healing times. When it comes to the physical, we stand at the edge of mystery.

Jesus contains the full mystery within himself in some way that I do not pretend to understand. Many creeds are written after Mark pens his gospel. Those creeds attempt to present the mystery of the Christ. All creeds fail in this effort. Faith recognizes the mystery.

The mystery touches a man's hand and the hand is restored. The Pharisees can only see the infraction of an old rule. They cannot even see the mystery. Jesus' anger is centered in their being so much in the dark when they are supposed to be those whose job it is to be sacred handlers of the mysteries of God.

MARK 3:7–12
THE CROWDS AND THE DEMONS

This is a scenario that most preachers would recognize: If you ask someone who comes to church on a certain Sunday, "How many people were there in church today?" they will give you a certain number. If you ask the preacher of that church the same question, the answer will have at least another fifty people added to it.

Mark tells us that Jesus departs to the sea with his few disciples (he has not called all of them yet) followed by "a great multitude from Galilee." No doubt that this is a large crowd, but because the followers are surging forward and jostling each other so much, it probably feels much larger. The reason for the numbers is the "new preacher," although Mark states that the people are gathering not so much because of what Jesus is saying but rather what he is doing. Everybody wants healing. This man can heal.

Your age will determine how you will picture the scene in these verses. My generation would use the image of *The Beatles* arriving in America. It is a mob scene. Jesus is a star and the crowd is mob-like.

Mark, as usual, does not go into great detail so one must pay attention to get the big picture. Jesus has his few disciples prepare a boat for his escape from the crowd. This sounds like a man who understands mob scenes. Jesus understands desperate people. The people who gather around Jesus do not want autographs. They long for something more personal. They desire healing.

At other times the crowd is interested in what Jesus is saying; today's mob is hungry for Jesus' touch. Word is out that he has "the power." At a time when there are no hospitals and few means of healing there is no way to imagine what these people must be feeling. There are many rumors about itinerant healers at that time, but this healer is for real.

Despite the fact that the crowd is eagerly pressing in, Jesus still has some work left to do and he does not want to be trampled to death by the crowd. He takes advantage of the boat that the disciples have prepared to give himself some space. Unlike some ideas that people have of Jesus, he does not and will not "leap tall buildings with a single bound." That is another character and not a real one.

Jesus is a very real person who is very special but not an unreal character. The prior sentence may sound like a bad translation of some original Greek, but what I mean is that he is divine but within human perimeters. Jesus is not some Superhero. He is a unique blend of human and divine. There are limits, and Mark's Gospel, being the one that was written closest to the time of Jesus, reveals some of those limits. Jesus needs some protection from the crowds.

It is obvious from the text that Mark believes in "unclean spirits" or demons. At that time in history, it was thought that demons caused mental illness but today we would not want to equate mental illness with demon possession. It can be very destructive and alienating to those who suffer from mental illness to be told that they are in some way demon-possessed. Nowadays we understand that mental illnesses have biological and social bases, rather than spiritual ones.

Much speculation has been brought forth as to whether Jesus believes in demons. Would not the divine Son of God know better than to participate in the mentality of his time? We can see that he uses language that indicates his belief in demons. God allows Jesus to be a child of his time. Whatever the case, the important thing is that Jesus is healing people in body, mind and spirit.

Mark of course would not know to think in these terms. For Mark the demons simply represent the powers that Jesus has come to defeat. Those who know *Star Wars* imagery can easily acknowledge and recognize "the power of the dark side of the Force." Jesus knows that there exists "a dark side" and he is well aware of the powers that bind, oppress, and exclude people. Today, demons may be thought of not as beings, but as anything which pushes against the healing, wholeness, justice, and love that God desires for individuals and for society as a whole.

In Mark's dealing with demons, the demons are the ones who first recognize who Jesus is. Jesus tells them, in this case, not to "come out" but to "be quiet." The demons are the strange light from the dark side which illuminates the outline of Jesus' messiahship. The demons are the foil against which Jesus is first seen.

It almost seems that Jesus wants the demons to be silent so that they won't spoil the surprise coming later. In Mark's Gospel, Jesus' suffering and servant leadership are primary, not his miracle-workings or his titles. The fact that the crowds are following Jesus because of his actions demonstrates what kind of Messiah the people are looking for. They are attracted by his "magic wand." The demons, by calling out that Jesus is the "Son of God," are more in tune with what Jesus is really about.

I preached a sermon one time at a small, rural church I was serving. The congregation consisted for the most part of farming people with minimal formal education who had gone to textile mills to make a living when farming no longer provided an adequate way of life. My own education was, in part, a hindrance to my efforts to communicate with them. One Sunday I decided to preach about "demons." I tried my best to show that today we need to understand the symbolic and metaphorical quality of demons in our own lives. To "name our demons" was the first step in allowing God to help us deal with them.

I spoke of greed, selfishness, pride, and obsessive individuality as some examples of "demons." The people seemed to really respond to the sermon. That was not always the case. Most of the people kept telling me that I was not preaching "hard enough." One big, strapping man had told me that "We don't need a preacher to remind us of how good we are. We need a preacher to tell us how bad we are."

In any case, this particular Sunday I seemed to have struck a receptive chord. I was feeling good until one enthusiastic man came out, shook my hand and said, "I'm glad you finally preached about them demons, preacher. I've got two of them in my closet." Some demythologizing is a waste of time. Jesus probably knew that before I did.

The crowd in these verses is clamoring around Jesus because he can manhandle the demons; the ones in their bodies and the ones in their closets. The crowd may be there for the wrong reasons (they aren't yet able to glimpse the larger picture), but they are there and in great numbers. Despite the fact that they are working for the dark side, the demons are the ones who are able to recognize Jesus' significance. In Mark's Gospel it seems that everybody is having a hard time understanding what Jesus is really about, including the disciples he is getting ready to choose.

MARK 3:13–19A
CHOOSING THE TWELVE

Jesus selects and then commissions. He does it in these verses and he does it today. The selection does not make those who have been appointed special, but it does make them needed. In Mark these twelve named disciples are not prominent characters. They are simply the ones chosen for the specific tasks of healing and proclaiming. Jesus needs help. It was and is that simple.

Those who are still waiting for Jesus to operate in a manner that is different from this are going to be left waiting. People have been waiting ever since he spoke the words of calling that we now have before us in these verses. Jesus makes it clear in these verses that he expects those whom he calls to do some definite things in his name. He will not do it all. He calls others to carry on his work.

It is interesting that the names of the twelve differ in different Gospels. What makes them special is not their names or their individuality, but their willingness to follow Jesus and do what he commands.

Amazing things can happen when ordinary people respond to the call of Jesus.

The text implies that a few of the twelve were distinguished by nicknames. These few have a reputation in the early church. Peter becomes "the rock," James and John are "the sons of thunder," the rowdy bunch, and Judas is "the betrayer," which is about as bad a nickname as you can get.

In Mark's Gospel, the disciples are, for the most part, background figures who help the story move along. Jesus is primary. In a day where individuality has become primary we need to again hear Mark's version of the story. There is a bigger plan. Jesus is primary. The community of believers is next. And coming in last is the individual. It seems that often in the modern-day church the order is reversed. Could it be that is part of our problem?

MARK 3:19B-27
JESUS AND BEELZEBUL: THE DEVIL MADE HIM DO IT

Now we reach an interesting few verses. Jesus returns "home." A crowd again gathers around him, but this time his family becomes concerned both for and about Jesus. Mark cuts to the chase and says that his family thinks he is mad. This time we are not talking about anger, we are talking about crazy.

Already we understand that Mark is presenting a Jesus who is not understood by the crowds. We have a Jesus who has set up Messianic expectations but who is going to present a far different picture than the one the Jewish people want. Now we have Jesus' own family thinking he has gone off the deep end.

What are members of his family expecting? We have no Christmas story in Mark where Jesus' mother goes through a virgin birth and is assured that her son is the one.

Why does Jesus' family now think his actions are crazy? Could it be that his own family is not ready for the radical nature of what he is doing and saying?

Why does Mary not stand up for her boy? Why does she not say, "He seems crazy because the ways of God *are* crazy. I ought to know"?

There is the temptation to mix the Gospels and try to explain one of them by using another. We simply cannot do it. Mark is using his own sources. We have to let the Gospel of Mark stand on its own whether we like the picture or not. Mark is telling about a man who is not even understood by his own family. A picture of growing isolation is being painted.

The religious leaders chime in and accuse Jesus of being possessed by the devil. Jesus counters with a kind of parable in which he says something along the lines of, "Why would the devil commit suicide by shooting himself?"

Oftentimes Mark does not give the reaction to what Jesus does. I for one would like to know what his family says about all this. Are they reassured by Jesus words? Do they share in the fear that he is possessed by some spirit?

Mark is saying clearly that being a follower of Jesus is not going to be easy. Being called crazy is going to be part of the package. Remember that the folks hearing Mark's Gospel for the first time are probably being called crazy for lining up to follow a crucified Messiah.

I often think that we domesticate and tame our modern version of Christianity, so perhaps we need to reintroduce the craziness of faith. There should be an element of faith that leaves one feeling a bit crazy. It is the part that makes us wonder if we are really going to follow a man who talks about "losing to find, dying to live, and forsaking all in order to have." Have we turned the sayings into poetry? Some of them *are* crazy. He intended them to be that way. This foolish craziness is the new way of life for a world whose "wisdom" has a bankrupt element within it.

The "over-againstness" of Jesus' words is met by the accusation of insanity by even his own family. Let us not lose this early reality that Mark preserves for us. Jesus is pushing against what people expect to be normative. The real spirituality of Jesus has a fire about it. Some religious practice attempts to contain the fire into a small flame to be placed in a lamp, a lamp for individual devotional reading.

Jesus comes to set the woods on fire. He once said that he came to bring fire to the earth. He is crazy. Within him burns the flame of God. His frame contains what has never been pulled off before or since. He is the "God-Man." He is a delicate balance of the divine and the human.

I wonder sometimes if such a high octane blend would not have felt crazy. Maybe what Jesus is really saying is, "Yes, I am crazy but it is not the devil that makes me so. The source is none other than my Father in heaven. Want to be crazy with me?"

Close examination often shows that family units have within them an internal kind of craziness that only the family can really comprehend.

Jesus offers those who will follow him an opportunity to be part of his family. His biological family has to realize that Jesus' understanding of family is much bigger than the family tree. Under the shade of Jesus' father's family tree there will stand all types of people. When the religious types of the day realize just how inclusive the shade of the tree will be, they know Jesus has to be crazy. Their solution is to either cut down the family tree or hang Jesus from one of its branches.

MARK 3:28–35
THE UNPARDONABLE SIN/JESUS' REAL FAMILY

Guilt is feeling bad about what you have done. Shame is feeling bad about who you are. Jesus expects that his followers will sometimes experience guilt because the expectations of being a disciple are challenging enough that guilt is sometimes the consequence, but Jesus has no room for shame. He has the divine quality of seeing each person as a child of God with infinite worth simply because *they are.* All the titles and good deeds are not important. Grace is the new norm by which people are measured. We all start the same, and we all mess up eventually. The law cannot save us. The many religious laws in Jesus' day that were intended to be life-giving so often led beyond guilt to shame.

Jesus offers forgiveness for sins, but in this passage we read Jesus' statement about an "eternal sin," sometimes translated as the "unpardonable sin," which is committed by "whoever blasphemes against the Holy Spirit." People who think that maybe they have committed the unpardonable sin experience all kind of shame. They may have a mental picture of a God who suddenly says at the Heavenly Gate, "Whoops, you can't get in. You committed the unpardonable sin and did not know it. Surprise!" This may be some kind of scary story that has haunted them from childhood.

In fact, if one listens closely to Jesus and watches closely how he lives and teaches forgiveness, one will wonder what this "unpardonable" sin might be. We hear the word "blaspheme" and we think of some kind of curse. A curse is usually thrown out to demean or disregard someone. It expresses a contempt or lack of reverence for God or something that is considered sacred.

In the context of Mark's Gospel, Jesus is referring to those who have just accused him of working for the powers of evil. These accusers feel threatened by Jesus and the way he is healing and freeing people. They do not want to accept that God may be working through someone outside of their system.

The accusers are also so much caught up in a sense of their own righteousness and superiority that they have lost the ability to distinguish good from evil. They have become incapable of recognizing the work of God when it is right before them, and do not appreciate that Jesus views each person as a sacred child of God, worthy of his attention. They are more concerned about judging, shunning, excluding and oppressing others.

Jesus' "Abba" has no room for such a way of treating people. Jesus comes to open the doors to people not to shut them, to free them, not to bind them. The religious leaders of Jesus' day who accuse him of conspiring with the dark side are getting real close to the unpardonable sin stuff because they are shutting down God's expansive grace and blocking off the family connection that is essential for the right understanding of life.

Jesus offers those who will listen to him a chance to re-establish this right relationship to God, but if a person has lost sight of moral vision, of right and wrong, of the dignity and respect that is due to every person, they may be unable to see a need to ask for forgiveness. They may say, "I do not need the Spirit of God. I am the captain of my own fate. What I have gained in life, I have made myself. It is all about me." This person may put himself or herself outside the family. God does not do this.

Family connection is important to Jesus. For him, "family" goes way beyond the concept of biological family. He says, "Whoever does the will of God is my brother and sister and mother." The real family of Jesus are those who express their reverence for God by their regard for others, and their actions towards them.

Jesus upset their theological apple carts. You can bet he is looking straight at them with those penetrating eyes of his when he uncharacteristically speaks of an unpardonable sin. Even this harsh statement has behind it the earnest desire to grant pardon and freedom to those who have shut the doors.

Chapter Four

MARK 4:1-34
PARABLES OF THE KINGDOM

Here is another reality that all preachers are aware of. In the midst of a sermon, if people start drifting away from you into sleep or some far distant
place that parishioners go while sermons are being offered, all you need do
is say, "Let me tell you a story." Heads quit nodding and eyes open.

People are walking stories. Life has a narrative quality to it. Mark's
Jesus is more a storyteller, miracle worker, and healer than he is a
preacher. There are no long sermons in Mark. The farther away one gets
from the time of the writing of Mark's Gospel, the longer Jesus' sermons
get. By the time you get to the Gospel of John, Jesus almost has three
points and a poem.

Arguments can abound as to what Jesus is really like. Does Jesus
speak in long discourses but Mark chose only to highlight needed elements for the sake of style or theology? Or is it that, as some biblical
scholars believe, Mark more adequately portrays the style of Jesus while
later Gospels offer more and more embellishment as the early church
uses Jesus to make their case for the faith?

Whatever the case, Mark's Jesus does not spend a lot of words.
Mark's Jesus does more than he says. These series of parables in chapter
four are a condensed version of Jesus' use of parables.

Many scholars think that Jesus' original parables were told quickly
and plainly and left for the hearer to interpret. Interpretations of parables
on the lips of Jesus may be the early church "preachers" doing a number
on the parables. Being a preacher myself, this makes sense. Our job is
to take what Jesus says and expound on its meaning for contemporary
living. Mark's church starts doing the same thing. In Mark's Gospel, we
may be looking over the preacher's shoulder while he is doing his work
of interpretation.

It all gets put together at the hand of Mark. To try to decipher which are Jesus' actual words and which are Mark's interpretations is a bit like drilling down through the layers of the Grand Canyon in order to get to the bottom of it. You might be able to do it, but why not just step back and enjoy the multi-layered portrait of collective history. It takes all those layers to make a canyon that is grand.

Efforts such as the recent Jesus' Seminar seem to be attempting to mine the Grand Canyon by lifting off layers, one at a time. What can happen with this is that you are left with piles of sediment on one side and no canyon after you finish. There is still water running by but the grandeur has been destroyed by too radical a reductionism.

It is good to do some excavation—we can gain some valuable insights from this type of work—but I would rather enjoy the canyon and its history painted in layers. Oh well, I have drifted into my own kind of parable of the canyon. Back to Jesus.

The first parable is a most famous one about the sower and the various soils. The parable of the soils is a preacher's gold mine. Not only is the original parable a clear version of how people respond to the words of the kingdom, but more so, Jesus' interpretation of the parable preaches the sermon for you.

The question behind the message of Jesus' announcement of a new kingdom is, "If this stuff is so good, why does not everyone respond favorably?" Rather than giving a sermon, Jesus tells a story that makes the point.

I love Jesus' stories. Sometimes they become a bit too familiar so that we do not do what he asks in the telling of them, "Those who have ears to hear, let them hear." Jesus uses things around him to make his point. The problem is that most of us are distant from agrarian lifestyles which include seeds, and sheep, and the mysteries of waiting for things to grow.

We need to re-see and re-hear the vivid nature of what Jesus is doing in his similes. For instance, when I preached one Sunday on the parable of the wise and foolish maidens, I dressed up like the Energizer Bunny and told the story of waiting too late to go buy batteries for my flashlight. A hurricane was predicted and I got busy doing other things and waited too late to prepare.

When I walked into the grocery story late that evening, it dawned on me, "Do you really expect there to be any batteries left in this town?" Sure enough when I arrived at the battery display, there was a big pink bunny whose cardboard belly used to hold batteries. What was in that belly? You got it, nothing.

Jesus' point of being prepared comes home because although my urban congregation could not relate to filling oil lamps and being ready, they could relate to that pink bunny who keeps "going . . . and going . . . and going." Jesus loves images and stories because he knows how the human mind works.

Within this chapter is the rather curious quote from Isaiah which Jesus uses to suggest that the reason people do not understand his parables is that their hearts are hardened by God so much that nothing will sink in. Jesus later states that, "Nothing that is hidden will stay that way; all will be revealed." What is happening here?

Does God harden the hearts of the people in my congregation so that they will not hear the Word? Perhaps in a roundabout way it does happen. God gives us freedom to choose to become too busy, too preoccupied, and too full to be able to take in the Word.

God offers chances for us to soak our hardened hearts in some life-giving water so that they can become receptive and soft. There is a mystery to this kingdom that Jesus is offering through Mark's words. That mystery is portrayed by a seed that does its work in secret while we go about our business. That mystery is revealed by looking at how small a mustard seed is and stating that "such is the kingdom." God's surprise is to use that which the world might judge to be small and insignificant to change the world.

Remember that by the time Mark pens his Gospel, rejection of Jesus' message has taken on momentum. If Jesus is the Messiah, then surely this rejection must also be part of God's plan. Another part of the plan is not only the rejection of the message of Jesus, but also the rejection of Jesus the man.

An itinerant healer/miracle worker will get himself crucified and offer that act as the new fulcrum upon which to rest the entirety of life. We have made this act too religious, too quick. The weakness of it is Mark's reason for writing his Gospel. He has to show how such an event of passion and suffering is God's mysterious way of saving all God's children.

Hearts will need to be soaked to understand such mysteries. No wonder so much of the message still does not produce harvest. In our fast-paced world we pave over paths which rush us to the next event.

We have so many competing loyalties that the rocks and shallow soils continue to produce exactly what they have always produced.

Jesus leaves us at the end of this series of parables with a mystery. Why do so many not respond? There is mystery to the gospel. There is supposed to be. This is a God thing. God is doing a new thing that will always have mystery to it because God's ways are not our ways. We cannot control the growth of God's seed, but its power is amazing even if it does have to struggle to produce its harvest.

MARK 4:35–41
JESUS QUIETS THE STORM

Viewpoint and perspective determine meaning. Consider, for example, the story of the three blind men who encounter an elephant. The blind man who first touches the trunk of the elephant thinks it is a snake, the man who touches the leg decides it is a tree, and the man who touches the huge belly assumes it is a boulder.

The story of Jesus quieting the storm is like this. It could be viewed as simply a miracle story where Mark is showing that this bearer of the new kingdom is able to rule over all of nature. On the other hand, it could be viewed as a parable of the early church, or indeed of any follower of Jesus who struggles to believe in the face of all the storms that come.

For those who see the story simply as a nature-miracle story, Mark's telling of it reveals that Jesus treats the storm the same way that Jesus treats the demons. The language used to quiet the storm is the same used to quiet the demons. Literally translated, Jesus says, "Hush up and be harnessed." Jesus is seen as master of all the powers that be. He is even capable of taming the dark side of nature. Jesus here is dealing with "the devil and the deep blue sea," and the story shows he is master of both.

As a story of faith, the picture focuses not on the storm but on the disciples' attitude and faith in face of the storm. Jesus is asleep in the very section of the boat designed for the pilot to steer the vessel. Remember that at least four of these new disciples are fishermen. They evidently watch Jesus sleeping for a while figuring that surely he will wake as the boat starts rocking back and forth. Jesus' role as pilot is fine with them but their pilot is asleep while it looks like they might all drown.

Perhaps Peter says to his younger brother Andrew, "Look at him. How can he sleep? He must not know as we know how treacherous these waters can be. He is the one who called us from our boats but we know the boats and the water. Maybe he needs to listen to us for a while. He may understand preaching but we understand this sea."

James and John might say, "Our father Zebedee would sure have his say if he saw this scene. We left him and the nets and followed this man who wants us to fish for men. Now our father would wonder what kind of fisherman have we left everything for, one who sleeps while his crew is about to perish at sea."

This kind of faith meets Jesus as a fear-filled group of disciples awake him with words that echo from the mouths of all who doubt God's providence, "Do you not care that we are perishing?"

Jesus wipes the sleep out of his eyes, looks at this tiny scared band, and talks not to them but to the sea. "Hush now! Be quiet!" Jesus rebukes the waters first and then turns to the disciples with another rebuke, "Why are you so afraid. Have you no faith?"

I can imagine Peter's fledgling faith responding with words like, "Faith! Those of us who grew up fishing on this sea are taught to pray while we struggle with the sails and the wind. What kind of faith is it that waits?"

Such a response, though unstated, is in the background as the story closes with the questioning phrase, "Who is he that the wind and the waves obey him?" This question is not posed for dramatic effect. It is a real question for these struggling disciples. The story shows that they have no idea who Jesus really is yet.

Even as events unravel around Jesus later, this same Peter who will call him "Christ" goes under the water for the third time. He drowns in his doubt and denial. I wonder if Peter remembers in the midst of his denial that dark night in Caiaphas' courtyard, this day on the sea when he doubts and wonders who Jesus is. How many other storms will come while their pilot seems to sleep?

Mark knows for his own church that the boat is taking on water. Many of Mark's hearers are probably wondering if Jesus cares for their condition. Jesus not only seems to be sleeping he seems to be gone from the scene. Mark's original hears of his Gospel need to hear Jesus words, "Take heart and believe—I am with you."

After the resurrection, this same community will need to know that even if the boat sinks, Jesus will not let any storm completely overwhelm them. He is the master of all, even death, that final storm feared by so many.

Chapter Five

MARK 5:1–20
THE GERASENE DEMONIAC

Mark must really like the story of the Gerasene demoniac. This writer of few words spends twenty verses on this one disturbed man. Commentators tell us that Mark's version of this story is cobbled together from multiple earlier versions. Maybe Mark likes this story so much because it makes for good press for Jesus. Here we have a demonstration of Jesus' power over nature, demons, and people all wrapped into one. Mark appears to be continuing his presentation of Jesus as the ruler of all nature.

The demoniac himself is a combination of Rosemary's Baby, the girl in the movie *The Exorcist*, and Frankenstein's monster. This poor soul is a demon buffet. A whole slew of unclean spirits have taken up residence in his battered frame.

Darkness likes to hide where there is no light or life. This man spends his days and nights hanging around the tombs, alone in the mountains. He has no human contact save the unsuccessful attempts to restrain him with shackles and chains. He breaks open these chains but cannot free himself from the demons infesting his soul. He cannot free himself from his isolation and desperate self-destruction.

No sooner than Jesus steps out of the boat arriving in Gerasene, he walks right up to the man without any hesitation and commands the demons to come out of him. Jesus, the bearer of life and light, goes to the place of darkness and death and throws light onto the demons, thus exposing their true nature, and freeing the man from his miserable existence. Like the wicked witch in *The Wizard of Oz* when the "deliverer," Dorothy, tosses water on her, the demons begin to reel and squeal their own version of "What a world, what a world!"

Jesus sends the demons into a herd of swine that are feeding on the hillside. The swine respond by rushing down a steep bank and drowning themselves in the sea. Incidentally, the guide on one of my trips to Israel pointed out the cliffs where this story is traditionally said to have taken place. He told me that they are now known as the Golan Heights. If this is the case, the land is still troubled territory.

This part of the story has a folktale quality to it and is probably to be understood figuratively. Jewish law considers swine to be "unclean" animals. It is prohibited to eat or even touch them. If the demons that are ousted from the man are to be sent anywhere, Jewish listeners to the story would find a herd of swine a fitting place. The Gerasene region is Gentile territory and as such is also considered ritually "unclean." If we focus on the folktale aspect of the story, we may see the man as representative of the "uncleanness" of the whole region.

I suppose it is possible that a herd of swine could suddenly be "spooked"—pardon the expression—and run off the cliffs into the sea at the very time that Jesus releases this poor man. The whole story is, however, rather troubling if taken literally. My earlier effort to allow Jesus to accept the common knowledge of his day to deal with demons, while perhaps knowing better, falls apart if this story is to be understood as factual.

In the telling of this story, Mark sets up a bookend situation. On one end we have Jesus' rejection by the "clean" religious leaders, and on the other the response of the so-called "unclean" Gentiles from across the sea. None of them appreciate Jesus' words or deeds. When the Gerasenes see the man that Jesus has restored to wholeness sitting "clothed and in his right mind," they beg Jesus to leave their neighborhood. Maybe they think that Jesus is bad for business. Mark is demonstrating that Jesus is becoming surrounded by people who are suspicious of his powers.

This demon-possessed man, to some extent, could represent anyone with an unhealthy addiction of any kind. Our demons lead us to places of death and convince us to take up residence there. We often refuse offers of help and give excuses when needed help comes near.

My friends in AA understand this story. They know the price of living with demons. They also know how release feels when the demons are named. They gather together in meetings and name the demons as often as they can. In so doing they send their demons into "the pig pit."

Many people who have struggled with the demons of addiction of any kind know full well how the pig pit looks and feels because they have been there. People gathered for an AA meeting applaud when a story of release is shared. If you listen carefully the applause may sound a bit like a whole group of pigs crashing into the sea.

Mark ends his story with the newly-released demoniac desiring to follow Jesus. Jesus tells him to go and tell the story of his release. Here we see a gradual shift in Mark. At last someone is told to go tell about Jesus instead of keeping it secret.

No wonder Mark likes the story so much. Jesus begins to let the cat out of the bag just after he lets the demons out of the man. Jesus is inching toward letting people in on the Messianic secret.

MARK 5:21–43
THE MIRACLE ON THE WAY TO A MIRACLE: THE HEALING OF JAIRUS' DAUGHTER AND THE WOMAN WITH A HEMORRHAGE

Have you ever been somewhere that is beautiful, and wonderful, and then had the privilege of returning there with someone who is visiting this location for the first time? Recently I had the chance to go back to a very special place, an island which used to accommodate a magnificent resort. The resort went bankrupt leaving the forces of nature to take back what they had previously possessed.

As I was sharing this rare treasure with my friend, I found myself hard-pressed not to spoil the surprise of encountering beautiful, crystal clear water, and sculpted lagoons which look like something in a movie scene of Paradise Island. I wanted to tell him all about the astonishing vistas he would see, but then I realized that part of the wonder was the experience of happening upon them for the first time. I tried to resist telling him everything in order to allow the new pilgrim to discover the mystical nature of this island for himself.

This is what Mark is doing in this last part of chapter five. Mark is standing on the other side of the Resurrection when he writes the Gospel. The secrecy motif that recurs in his Gospel (in these verses, for example, he has Jesus give instructions not to pass on the news of the healings) is part of his way of holding back from telling about the wondrous event that Jesus would bring: the inauguration of a new kingdom whose reign announced victory over death.

Mark, even with his sense of urgency, now tells this impressive story of how Jesus overcame death—not that of his own, but of Jairus' daughter—but within the story, he pauses. Mark offers a dramatic interruption which is a window to the whole Jesus story.

The story begins as Jesus hears the plea of Jairus to come and save his daughter, who is on the point of death. Jairus is the leader of the local synagogue, which means he is a very important person. This one episode shows that Jesus' reputation has spread. Jairus is willing to take a chance on this healer.

Mark interrupts this story to tell the marvelous story of a woman who is lost in the crowd. She is a woman who is hopeless and "unclean." She has spent her resources on doctors. If the people in the crowd knew her problem, they would part like the waters of the sea. She is outside the help of the medicine of her day, and beyond the grasp of the religion of her times. Her hemorrhage makes her untouchable.

She moves stealthily through the crowd like some kind of assassin. She plots her course to gain access to this important figure who is being guarded by the disciples like so many Secret Service agents. The disciples are trying to get Jesus to his destination. They are doing their best at crowd control while allowing this popular figure whom they serve to have as much access to the crowd as possible.

Our woman, whom Mark now focuses on, attempts to make her move. She may only have one shot so she chooses her time. She carries no weapon in her hand. She carries a handful of empty hope. She holds in her heart the concept of taking life, but she wishes this famous personage no harm. She simply wants to take life from him so that she might gain life.

She touches his garment. The disciples push Jesus forward trying to get him to the really big miracle. Jesus stops their movement. He feels the shot. He knows that something has found the mark. No one else hears, feels, or sees the deed.

Jesus asks his Secret Service guys, "Who touched me?" He knows that life has been taken. I can just hear Peter, who loves to talk, responding, "Who touched you? Here we are trying to get you through this mob scene and you want to know who touched you? Give me a break. Do you know something we don't know?"

The answer to that question is "Yes." Jesus then makes this unnamed woman someone whom we will never forget. The crowd parts as if she indeed is an assassin. The very thing she fears happening now happens. She is caught.

This desperate woman, who can already tell that she has taken some of this man's life into her own, drops down at his feet. For the first time in years, what now flows in her is not an unclean stream of blood but a healing fountain. She kneels before this healer and she trembles with a strange mixture of gratitude and terror.

She confesses her plot. No one knows of her healing but her and the one from whom she has taken a portion of life-giving power. Some of the crowd still knows her only as "that woman," the unclean one, a hopeless case. She is found out, but somehow it does not matter, for in her poor tired frame, she senses that she is found after being so lost.

She does not look up into her accuser's eyes. She bows before such raw power as anyone would bow before some god. Her mind may not yet know who he is, but her body tells her he is divine. If her healing is only for this moment, after so many years of pain and shame she will take it. If he is to somehow condemn her for the assassin-like deed, so be it. She waits while the crowd murmurs.

Jesus now names and claims her. "Daughter, your faith has made you well." Mark uses the Greek word "soza" in this story for the verb "to make well." This word can also be translated as "to save"; in this case Jesus ties the woman's healing to her leap of faith. Her faith saves her and makes her whole. Jesus sends her walking through the crowd, a broken woman now made whole, and he says as she departs, "Go in peace." He gives her the blessing of shalom.

We are now waiting in anticipation of what will happen to Jairus' daughter. In the same way that I wanted my friend on the island to experience the surprises for himself, Mark wants us to find out the wonder of a new reality in stages. The joy of resurrection is anticipated. But now Jesus discovers that the little girl is dead.

No point in going on. Jairus might want to shake the poor woman who has just been healed. "If it were not for you and your plotting, my little girl might have been helped by this Jesus."

Jairus' friends all start the traditional moaning and groaning which is customary and traditional at the time of death. Jesus interrupts them with the announcement that "She is only sleeping." They all laugh at him and start back up with the moaning and groaning. Jesus steps through the groaning crowd and simply tells the little girl to "Get up; it's time to go play."

As Jesus walks through the crowd of mourners who no longer know what to do, he turns, smiles, and says, "By the way, get the child something to eat." Like my island experience, there is beauty in the middle of a bankrupt situation. Mark lets us in on the anticipated paradise but he makes us wait with dramatic pauses. Mark has been to the island. Some of his first readers have not.

We who know what the island looks like must be careful not to take it for granted. There are still those who have not witnessed its wonders. The surprise is wonderful. The Lord who knows the touch of those who are hopeless, the one who tells doubt-filled people to go fix a peanut butter and jelly sandwich for a child who was as cold as a stone a few moments earlier, this Lord is the Lord of life and of death. Mark loves to tell the story even as he makes us wait for its triumphant conclusion. It is a conclusion that will happen at an empty tomb.

Chapter Six

MARK 6:1-6
JESUS REJECTED IN HIS HOME TOWN

One of my Sunday school teachers used to make us call out a Bible verse instead of responding "Present" when the attendance roll was called. Methodists are not notorious for memorizing Bible verses so most of us scrambled to recite the shortest verse in the Bible, "Jesus wept." before anyone else got to it.

"Be ye doers of the word and not hearers only." was a close second. For me however, there was another verse that lodged in my shallow memory bank, "A prophet is not without honor except in his own country." It was short enough, but it also velcroed itself to my childhood flannel board because it seemed strange to me.

Why would a prophet not be honored in his own country, especially if the prophet was Jesus? Why would Jesus' hometown not be plastered with signs along the road reading, "Hometown of Jesus the Christ—Savior of the World"?

If I were a Presbyterian with a strong inclination to the concept of predestination, I would have a theological reason for remembering this short verse about rejection. My first appointment as a United Methodist pastor was to a church in my hometown. The assignment was not in my home church, but it was the town where I grew up.

Jesus' words came flashing back. Suddenly I saw their meaning. I wondered if I would be greeted with remarks such as "I knew you when you were in the Scout program," or "Were you not the one who dropped that pass on the goal line?" or "Wasn't your home church that church from across the tracks that is drying up on the vine now?"

Familiarity has its limitations and bindings. It can be an asset if people allow it to be, but the agenda can be set for you by the time you arrive. People's expectations have been prejudiced by their own view of the past. This could be the receptive field for planting seeds of "local boy makes good," but some people do not want the local boy to make good.

Some people cannot believe that heroes are people they know. Heroes are supposed to be larger-than-life figures, not people like us. There is supposed to be some defining quality that makes them special that could not have come from the same air that *we* breathe. This kind of thinking may actually be some strange self-protection device to keep us from the necessary hard work of growth toward being better people.

Whatever the case, Jesus' "Welcome Back Party" is a flop. Maybe it is because word gets out that his own family has real concerns about his emotional stability. His reputation is definitely elevating him to star status, but the local folks have probably also heard of a growing momentum by the religious leadership to make Jesus a falling star. It seems that there is not room enough in the night-time religious sky for Jesus' constellation. The religious leaders have already mapped out their star charts and Jesus is not in the plan.

Jesus keeps talking about a new light. The religious leaders seem to want to keep people in the dark.

Jesus finally comes down on the side of not being able to have it both ways. According to Jesus, either you have to be willing to squint a bit and look at a new sun or you are going to be left in the dark. Jesus says it better than my meager words. He uses those previously mentioned images of new wine and old wineskins, and the image of a new patch sewn on an old garment.

The people in Jesus' hometown probably are not overly enthralled by the religious leadership of the day, but these leaders are all that they have. People have a hard time letting go of the old even though the old is not what they want. The uncertainty of the new can make one aware of just how secure one becomes with the old ways.

The times, for Jesus contemporaries, are filled with great insecurity and uncertainty. The Romans have them by the necks economically and politically. The religious establishment has them caught between attempting to keep laws they can not keep and waiting for a deliverer who has to fit a certain, very rigid, set of guidelines. Many people are afraid to take too many chances.

From the get-go, Jesus speaks about taking chances. The kids in Jesus' hometown, with whom he played on those childhood days after the chores were done, have a hard time believing that this same "Mary's kid" is the one they are supposed to take a chance on.

We who know the end of the story may think the people in his home town are really stupid. He offers them healing, but they are too busy hanging around the coffee shop gossiping about various rumors. The tabloids have already done their work. Headlines are already imprinted in some of their minds such as, "Local Carpenter Turned Healer Is Possessed by Legions of Demons," or "Child Brought Back from Death Discovered to Be Hoax."

The local folks have seen this boy work with wood. Those same people have listened to this local speak of one who will "save his people Israel and release captives from oppression." It is not that the local folks are opposed to being set free. It is just that this one whom they know so well can not possibly be the hoped-for hero. My God, this is Mary's kid after all.

Joseph is not mentioned by Mark, which could mean all sorts of things. It could be a veiled reference to a virgin birth; a birth which Mark does not mention. It could be a reference to a suspicious cloud around Jesus' birth which would make it hard to believe that this "out-of-wedlock" child is God's Messiah.

The absence of Joseph could simply mean that Joseph is already dead. Many people did not live long back then. Life was hard. If that was so, then some undoubtedly would have asked themselves, if Jesus is who some said he is could he not have kept his own father alive long enough to behold such wonders?

The questions obviously have a snowball effect. By the time Jesus comes to his own, his own receive him not. There are too many questions and too many problems with his short biography. Jesus does not fit the hometown folks' profile for Messiah. The people in his original neighborhood know this reality better than the crowds.

The people in his home town know who he is. He is all too human to them. They have a hard time believing that this very familiar figure could possibly contain the essence of divine hope.

In the church of today, this story could be a parable of those who know Jesus too well. The Jesus' story sometimes becomes theological muzak in the local church. We hear it, but it does not really seep into our souls where it can make a difference. The muzak music is not stirring. It no longer moves us or brings tears to our eyes. We hear something like the Prodigal Son story, and we say, "Oh yeah, that's the Prodigal Son story." We miss the pathos of a broken-hearted father, the rather good reasons for the envy of an elder brother, and the truly lost boy who still smells of pigs. It becomes "The Prodigal Son story."

We who have grown up in the church know Jesus well. Sometimes the crowd outside can see him and hear him better than we can. To them he is novel, even interesting. The crowd outside the "home" of the church might be more aware of their emotional and physical hungers than us church folks who have become used to literal and emotional covered dishes.

It is still hard to pour new wine into old wineskins. Surely the church does not become like those old wineskins? It happens, and when it does, Jesus is listened to in his hometown but he is not really heard. And if he is not really heard, he is not honored, for honoring Jesus means taking chances and being willing to be really changed.

Familiarity can be a safeguard against "dying in order to live." Jesus offers death in the face of old ways. We still do not like to talk of death.

I wonder if Jesus still marvels at our lack of faith much like he does that day in his hometown. I think there are times we need to go ahead and pour the new wine into the old wineskins and let the breaking-open happen. Things often get too stiff and stale in the church. The signs out front of our towns might in fact read, "Hometown of Jesus Christ," but if the power of new wine is not present then the honor he spoke of is missing.

Jesus is not interested in museums with artifacts telling an old story. He is interested in making people whole, naming demons, and calming storms.

It is still a short Bible verse but one worth remembering. To truly honor Jesus in the land he claims as his own can be a really scary thing. Our demons start shaking in the presence of the kind of freedom Jesus offers because we become comfortable with our demons. Our wineskins begin to stretch when this new wine enters. We may start wondering if we have bitten off more than we can chew.

To "honor Jesus in his own country" may leave us feeling not so much at home. Jesus has a way of calling those who will follow him to come away from comfortable, familiar places. His first disciples discover this reality as we shall see in the next section. Disciples who choose to follow Jesus today often discover that he still bids us to leave the comfort of "home."

MARK 6:7–13
THE MISSION OF THE DISCIPLES

Until now in Mark's Gospel, the disciples seem to be struggling to understand just who Jesus is and what their own role is. Suddenly—a lot happens suddenly in Mark—their role is made crystal clear for them. Ready or not, they are sent out like new salesmen who are to learn about selling by selling. Jesus throws them in the deep water and from the shore line yells, "Swim!"

The disciples are like soldiers being sent into battle with no armor. Their enemies are the same demons that Jesus has gotten to know on a first-name basis. Now, it is one thing for demons to shake in their boots at the sight of Jesus, but why should they bother to turn their minds from their appointed tasks at the sight of one of Jesus' disciples?

If the devil has done his homework, he would think he has nothing to fear from this tiny band of would-be followers of Jesus. They lack faith, understanding, and courage. Is this going to be like sending boys to do men's work? Is it going to be like sending children with slingshots into the field with the enemy who possesses artillery?

Jesus for sure has done *his* homework. He knows the story of David and Goliath. He was teethed on the story of Gideon and little band of men defeating the many. Jesus' battle plan is taken from the pages of the manual written by the Chief of Staff. Pharaoh's heavy chariots are about to get bogged down again in the sea. Traveling light has its advantages.

The disciples are told to take only minimal provisions and clothing. They are to rely on the power that Jesus will send with them. They are going to show the rest of us that "If I can do it anyone can." The disciples are not painted in the best light by Mark, but they pull it off.

The demons do discover that these wimpy newcomers possess the very power that is supposed to emanate only from the bearer of the new kingdom. Somehow being sent out "in his name" confers a type of ambassador status on the one who is willing to be obedient to the discipline of Jesus.

The power Jesus offers these disciples seems to be based on certain conditions. They should go in twos for support. They cannot rely on security to keep them secure. Jesus has them leave almost everything behind. They are only allowed the shirts on their backs and a suitcase big enough for one day's needs.

This is going to be a spiritual *Outward Bound* experience. It is time for the disciples to come back from their experience different because they have learned to rely on their own resources and the power of the resources around them. They are going to have to trust their leader and be willing to rough it.

Jesus takes some of the burden off their shoulders because he tells them that they are not responsible for getting any kind of quota on healing and soul-saving. They are simply to proclaim the message and offer the power. If that message is not received, or the power not effective, he tells them they should "shake the dust off their shoes" and move on. Jesus will be responsible for the numbers game. If it does not work, it is his problem, not theirs. Their task is to be obedient to the rule.

In our modern-day church of statistics and goals, Jesus' words seem almost alien. First of all, traveling as "light" as he requests sounds like a strange arrangement to the present-day church. What would I do without my laptop and power point presentation? How effective would I be without the briefcase full of books that I bring to get my message across? And this part—about carrying no bread, no bag, and no money?—well indeed, Jesus needs some instruction in our contemporary situation. Programs cost money. My diet requires good healthy food. Relying on Jesus alone for my material when there are so many good books around seems most foolish.

Yes, we have come a long way—perhaps too far. Reading Jesus' words today and hearing again of the disciples' success at healing, proclaiming, and taming demon spirits, armed only with his promise and the shirt on their backs, jerks a knot in my soul. There is nothing wrong with equipping oneself for ministry—I talk about it all the time and believe in it—but the bottom line is that we need to have a deep reliance on the promise and power of Jesus.

The danger is that in the midst of all our money and resources we will get too far away from Jesus' promise that all that we need to possess in order do his work will be provided. Maybe the demons do not shake like they used to because what they see is modern-day disciples trying to do Jesus' work with various pieces of equipment rather than simply relying on the promise of the Master that all will be provided.

Jesus still makes promises about the power that will be available in his name, but he also still wants to see whom and what we are depending on. If we are depending on programs and resources for our main source of power, the demons smile because they know a lot of our tricks of the trade. I have a feeling that what makes those same demons shudder today is when they see a disciple, who is perhaps a bit naïve but nonetheless starry-eyed, with the attitude that maybe they can accomplish the task they have set their mind to, if they stick to the orders from headquarters.

Let us remember though, that Jesus has spent time with his original tiny band first. He has gotten to know them and they are beginning to get to know him. And even if they do not yet fully understand him they are willing to give it a go in his name. Amazing things happen when they do just that. Spending time with Jesus and getting to know him even in the midst of struggling to believe is still important in this disciple thing. Amazing things still happen when people rely on Jesus first and their resources second. Sometimes we discover that we do not even need our laptops.

MARK 6:14–29
THE DEATH OF JOHN THE BAPTIST

Getting cut from the team is a sad feeling. I remember the year when I went against all odds—and most of my feelings—and tried out for the high school varsity basketball team. I was a decent football player, and besides, almost nobody was cut from the football team, but basketball involves fewer people. Mistakes cannot be hidden under equipment and crowds. In basketball you are exposed.

The chances were slim that I was going to make it onto the team. Surprisingly I made it through the first few cuts. The team had to get down to fourteen people. It had already been pared down to sixteen. Everybody knew who would be the next ones to go: Stanley and me. We might as well have had "cut me" printed on our practice shirts.

The fateful day came. As the coach dismissed practice, he simply said, "Could I see Jody and Stanley for a moment?" Our "friends" on the team all started walking away. When they were positioned behind the coach, they turned and together they mimed slitting their throats, indicating to us that the cut was about to happen.

They did it in fun, but we knew they were right. We made the coach's job easier by telling him, before he had even got the words out, that we had decided to drop off the team because our studies were more important than silly old basketball. He laughed and we did too. It made the cut a little less painful.

John the Baptist is cut from the team. His cut is very painful. Mark spends a good number of words telling the story. The story seems to come out of the blue. There has been little mention of John. Mark has just been telling the story of the disciples' efforts at healing and proselytizing. Why now this dramatic story of John being cut?

Mark evidently wants to foreshadow not only Jesus being cut from the team, but also the eventual cutting of the disciples by those coaches of the world who simply will not have the likes of them playing on their teams. Remember that Mark writes this story after the crucifixion has taken place, and in the midst of opposition to the faith by all sorts of powers. Mark uses this account of the death of John the Baptist to show how the world will reject the message before it accepts it.

John, who is already a hellfire-and-damnation kind of prophet, steps over the line when he accuses Herod of committing adultery by marrying his brother's wife. You can imagine that such talk does not go over well at the local bridge club. Herod's wife knows what the other women are whispering about and she is overheard one day saying, "I'll have that —'s head."

King Herod is evil and cruel—according to historical accounts— but he is not stupid. Herod knows that John has a big following and is considered a righteous man. Since Herod's plaque over his throne room reads: "Herod: King of the Jews," he has at least to act like he observes and respects the religion of the Jews.

John has been screaming about repentance and the coming of the Messiah. Will Herod cut off one who may as well have been promoting mom and apple pie? Herod does not completely need the people behind him, but neither does he need a messy religious revolt. The Romans allow him to serve. The Romans and Herod have a deal which is a little like the deal a tick has with a dog. You find both together but one sucks life and the other scratches. Who is the dog and who is the tick depends on who you are talking to and who is listening.

Herod arrests John in order to shut him up. Herod after all does have to live with his wife—although he has been known to cut wives too. Throwing John in a dingy cell seems like a good compromise. John's righteousness will still be upheld and there is biblical precedent for punishing prophets.

The trouble comes, as it often does, when Herod has a little, or maybe a lot, too much to drink at his birthday party. He gathers all his cronies together for the party. Herod's wife's daughter, who is evidently quite a looker, dances in front of the party and in Herod's face. Her night job must be at the *Leather and Lace Men's Club* because she knows how to gain a man's attention when she dances.

Between Herod's lusty looks, too many drinks, and a wife who knows what she wants, Herod is had. He stands up and with a drunken slur says, "Honey that was some dance. I'll give you anything you want."

The sweet young thing bats her eyes, looks over at her smiling mom, and pops up with, "I'll have the head of John on a platter, please." Herod swallows his tongue, coughs as if a drink has gone down the wrong way, and realizes that the goose that he and his cronies have just consumed for the birthday party is not the only goose that is cooked.

The entrapped Herod has to make good on his drunken promise in order to save face with the crowd. The crowd probably thinks that cutting John is a great idea since some of them have been mentioned by name in John's previous sermons.

John is cut from the team. The drama ends with his head on a platter. He is delivered like cold pizza to a smiling dancer.

Mark wants us to stop and take notice. This same thing is going to happen to Jesus. Jesus himself is going to be delivered up. While at this point in Mark's story Jesus is being received with interest by large groups of people, Mark is preparing the reader for a coming change. Mark wants us to pay close attention because rejection is creeping its way into the story like water seeping under the door in the face of a coming flood.

The story ends for John. The cut is final. The story will soon seem to end for Jesus too. The powers that be will brush their hands together, or wash their hands as the case may be, and say, "Now that's that!" But the cut will not be final. Jesus, unlike John, will show up three days after the cut and scream out, "Play ball!"

This solitary proclamation will reach the ears of Herod, and Pilate, and all kinds of religious leaders after they have already cut out the lights in the gym and are standing around in the parking lot. They will laugh and pat each other on the back and say, "You know, that sounded like him, didn't it?" But they will go on thinking that the cut is final.

I am writing these words now only because the observations made by these coaches are wrong. Herod eventually runs out of birthday parties, Pilate never really can get his hands clean, and the religious leaders find out what all that new wine does to their old wineskins. Jesus is cut like John, but this is Jesus: the bearer of a kingdom whose rule and power John only alluded to. Jesus is the beginning of a kingdom without end. Herod, and those like him, will discover that it is hard to cut such power.

MARK 6:30–44
FEEDING THE FIVE THOUSAND

Jesus understands the need for an ebb and flow to discipleship. He recognizes the need for a time to work and a time not to work. When his disciples come back from their first sales trip, Jesus looks into their eyes and sees both the joy of success and the tiredness of having done something spiritually hard for the first time.

After all, these men who are fishermen, craftsmen, a tax collector or two, a rebel, and who knows what else, have never claimed to be exorcists or preachers. Jesus commissions them to do both. Evidently their journeys out into the countryside two by two are mostly successful.

When the disciples return from their assigned journeys, they are like excited children who conquer a task for the first time and beg a parent with the words, "Oh, can we do it again? Please?" Jesus, however, knows what is waiting ahead. Things will not always be so successful. Maybe the disciples haven't paid close attention to rejections by family and hometown peers. Mark portrays Jesus' disciples as being somewhat oblivious to impending danger signals.

As the disciples tell about their daring feats, Jesus looks into their eyes and says to them, "Come away by yourselves to a lonely place and rest a while." These are words of wisdom from a man who understands the pattern of activity and rest.

In modern-day discipleship we often lose this sense of balance between activity and rest. In my work as a pastor I see people who often "grow weary in well doing" and get bitter when their efforts either are not appreciated or are misunderstood. On the other hand I see a lot of people who have, so to speak, bought a Jesus T-shirt, but who rest from the needed labors most of the time. Having the T-shirt does not mean you act on the cause. Some church folks seem to be on a perpetual sabbatical without having put in the years to merit the time off.

Jesus understands the need for getting the job done and the need for charging one's batteries. He calls his disciples to be right in the middle of the crowds, but he also calls them away to a quiet place. Being quiet with Jesus is not being selfish. Being quiet while in the presence of Jesus is a quality investment, if you want to do the discipleship thing.

We need to trust Jesus on this one. He knows that the discipleship thing is both joyous and draining. Quiet places are good investments for those who want to be disciples.

However, even Jesus becomes a victim of the "good intentions" syndrome. He wants to get away to a quiet place with his tiny band, but the crowds will not have it. Mark portrays the crowd as being like so many paparazzi who seem to be one step ahead of Jesus and his disciples.

Unlike some of the movie stars or other famous people who push away the clamoring, clutching crowd, Jesus sees the crowd as "sheep without a shepherd." Mark says that even though Jesus gives the "Let's get away and rest a while" speech, Jesus turns and starts in again teaching the crowds because he "had compassion on them." The disciples could come back at Jesus with the accusation that he must mean, "Do as I say not as I do." It is hard being Jesus. How's that for theological insight?

Yes, Jesus knows the need for rest, but he also knows he only has a short time to get done what needs to be done. Perhaps Jesus has in mind sending off the disciples for a rest while he takes care of things. Jesus has whispered that line in my "spiritual ears" a few times. "You go take a break. I'll handle things back here." I still have trouble trusting Jesus on this one. I must either think that I am indispensable, or that Jesus cannot really do it without me, or maybe other folks need this rest but I do not.

Anyway, in this story before us, Jesus and the disciples get caught up again with the crowd. Jesus teaches them on the spot. He always has a sermon in his pocket and a miracle up his sleeve. I do not mean that disrespectfully. He simply does.

Just about the time we get caught up in a biblical story to the point that it becomes fantastically religious and pious-sounding, Mark brings us back to earth with a very human element. The crowd gets hungry.

This is a great time for a covered dish meal. Some biblical observers think that is exactly what happens. Noting that all the people gathered are not stupid and that they know there are no *Handy Pantries* down by the lake, some observers think that what happens in this miracle of feeding the five thousand is that the people, who would have brought some food with them, simply share what they have with each other.

That is not the way Mark tells the story. In the background is Mark's theological motif. That background is one of Jesus breaking bread and giving hungry people what they need. Mark is getting ready to tell a story about Jesus walking on water so what is the big deal about him miraculously turning five loaves and two fish into baskets full of leftovers?

I personally have no idea what really happened that day. All of us preachers have joked about the five loaves and two fish when we are faced with limited resources. Many of us religious professionals, while holding our limited resources in hand, state glibly, "Well Jesus did the five loaves and two fish thing, but then, that was Jesus."

The real point of the story is just the opposite. In our present moments, if we trust Jesus and step out in faith, things can happen in a mighty way using the limited resources we have. Heck, it happens to me all the time. If I whine about not having enough, I always end up not having enough. If I take the limitations I have and offer them in spite of the way things are, amazing things happen. I have run to get baskets for the leftovers more than once.

However Jesus achieves this miracle, it must be very important to Mark. He ends up telling the same story in a different version later in his book. The tune must have played well in Mark's day.

This story of Jesus taking little and making much of it became larger than life for Mark's audience. Who knows exactly what actually happened on the midnight ride of Paul Revere, but what ended up happening was that the story became a symbol of courage and vigilance.

The story of Jesus feeding the multitudes becomes a symbol for Mark's church. The symbol is that even though times look tough and they have few resources, with Jesus it will all come out in the end. As in the story of Jesus calming the storm, Mark's church not only needs to know that Jesus is going to be with them in the boat when things get rough, but they also need to know that Jesus will be with them in the pantry when the shelves end up almost empty.

Soon the most important food for disciples in the first century will not be five loaves and two fish but one loaf and a small cup. Both will be served by Jesus the host.

In another version of the Jesus story told by another Gospel writer, Jesus says to the tempter, "Man does not live by bread alone." On this particular day by the lake, he lifts up bread and says the same thing, but this time he gives them some bread. Later he will say as he holds up a loaf of bread, "This is not bread alone—take and eat—it's me."

When bread is broken in Jesus' name, especially in the face of limited resources, and love is offered, amazing things can still happen. Multitudes are affected one way or another.

MARK 6:45–52
JESUS WALKS ON THE SEA

I am not sure what purpose is served by having Jesus walk on water—but then satisfying my concerns is not what occupies the focus of the Gospel of Mark. Walking on water almost fits in with one of those temptations offered to Jesus in another Gospel. The devil could have easily said, "Okay, there is the Dead Sea over there. I'll gather a crowd and you simply walk across to the other side. You can do that, can't you?"

Is this Jesus showing off? The very one who, in Mark's version of the Jesus' story, seems to be modest about his title and power, now walks across the waves in the presence of a group of wide-eyed disciples?

All kind of theories abound about this walking on water story. No, none of them with any credibility implies that Jesus "knew where the rocks were." That is no theory. It is an old, bad joke. Some theories mention this being an "epiphany" story which may have as its origin a time when Jesus walked up to the disciples by the sea and stepped into their boat to calm them down again in the face of angry waves.

Some speculate that the story is to be taken at face value. Jesus simply goes down to the edge of the sea and keeps walking. Quantum physics, the part I understand—which is a very small part—has some insights that are mind bending. Time changes and is bent inward at the speed of light. Two things can be in the same place at the same time. Reality is affected by the observation of reality.

The smarter we get the more we realize that there is more than meets the eye when we look into the nature of reality. The walking on water story is a watershed—pardon the expression—when it comes to your personal Christology. Christology is that part of your personal theology which deals with how you view Jesus.

Some people in the Christian faith act as if all of our Christology is the same or needs to be the same. A good deal of Christian history depicts this cookie cutter kind of thinking. Various creeds attempt to pour Jesus into a mold. It is and is supposed to be harder to do this than one might at first think.

Jesus, being "God's only begotten son," has a good deal of mystery surrounding him. Jesus is the human face of God, but this is still God we are dealing with here. Just about the time we think we have Jesus figured out, he may just slip through our fingers. Those who need him to be very human do not like this walking on the water stuff. It makes him too unreal, too magical, and maybe even too hokey.

For those whose Christology is filled with divine needs, Jesus walking on water is no big deal. Those persons wish we had more stories of him doing such deeds. They also may wish we had the pictures of him doing it.

Maybe the reality of it all depends on just how much Jesus participates in the human plane and how much he is part of the divine dimension. Even the science we can somewhat hold in our hands is telling us of possibilities that are beyond what some of us think can really happen. Jesus participates in both the divine dimension and the human one in a very mysterious fashion. I sure do not understand.

What is important to me is that Jesus walks toward those disciples who need him. He does not let "hell or high water" stop him. It is comforting to know that Jesus will not let a little thing like an angry sea stop him from crawling in the boat with a group of needy disciples.

In some religious traditions the faithful walk across a bed of burning coals and are not burned. Jesus walks across the water not to prove the faith but simply to get to the frightened group for whom he cares. He still does.

Mark ends this story by stating that "they were utterly astounded, for they did not understand about the loaves, but their hearts were hardened." They do not understand the loaves. They do not understand the walking on the sea. Hey, we are in good company. Anybody understand these two stories?

Are our hearts hardened? Do we have religious cataracts so that we cannot see? Mark's theology is stating that the reason the disciples do not get it is that the hardening is part of God's plan. This is Mark's only way of explaining how a group of people so close to Jesus just keep on not getting it. God intends it to be that way.

Mark is expressing his theology. I am not sure we have to agree with it. There is, however, something to be said with the words "They did not understand." We do not have to understand everything in order to believe.

Somehow, in some way, Jesus walks on the water and it is remembered as important. I think it means he gets to those who need him anyway he can with whatever means necessary.

MARK 6:53–56
A SWEEPING CONCLUSION

My Hebrew professor used to give excited speeches about the power of the Old Testament, painting his stories with broad strokes. At the end of class he would often say, "All generalizations are false, including this one." Mark is making a generalization in these last few verses of chapter six. If you read only these verses, you would think everything is going along fine. The crowds are both awed and pleased. Everyone is getting healed just by touching the fringe of his cloak. Everything is coming up roses.

Mark is summarizing in a hurry. He wants to move on to more controversy. He wants to show how, in spite of all the evidence, the powers of the day are not going to listen to or accept Jesus. It is part of the plan.

Mark is simply setting us up. Things are getting ready to get really interesting. The drama is building. If you did not already know the end of the story you would be asking some questions by now. Remember, some people who read Mark did not know the end of the story. When Mark gets them to the end of the story, he wants them to have had quite a ride.

Chapter Seven

MARK 7:1-23
KEEPING THE RULES AND KEEPING THE FAITH

I still remember his trembling lip. He was trying to convey the level of his anger. "Did you see what she did?" I did not know who he was referring to, or what the terrible deed was.

My apparent ignorance and lack of perceptivity seemed to make him even angrier. I was, after all, the preacher, and it was my appointed duty to keep things straight in the small rural church to which I was appointed. The large man with the trembling lip was the Lay Leader of this family church and he wanted to know why I was not outraged.

To his deep regret I had to ask him to draw me a picture. He described the few moments earlier when a young girl had walked past the two of us, stopped and made some idle comment, and then proceeded on out the door. We had just finished Wednesday evening choir practice in the Sanctuary when this "abomination of the holy" had occurred.

This young girl was wearing shorts. The shorts were not particularly short, especially in terms of how short shorts would become a few years later.

This man pointed to where the young girl had been standing. "You know what I am talking about." I had to get him to enlarge the picture. Having to state what was so obvious to him, but not significant to me, made this leader of the church wonder just who he had for a preacher.

He was upset because she had worn shorts in the sanctuary. I really wanted to say, "You must be kidding?" but I had been pastor of this little church long enough to know he was most serious. That was the problem. He was serious.

I knew something of this teenager's life. She came from a rough background and had something of a bad reputation. And now . . . and now she had the audacity to wear shorts in the "holy of holies."

When I finally got the picture this angry man was painting for me, I wanted to either cry or literally shake him. What I wanted to say was, "My God, you are concerned about her exposed legs? You are so caught up in some thwarted religious customs that you are wrapped too tight to really feel human need. At least this struggling child of God is here. Who gives a damn what she is wearing?"

I did not say this. I do not remember what I said. I was stunned. Knowing me, I probably wimped out and told him I would speak with her later about her clothing.

Looking back over the years at this event, part of me wishes I had said what I was thinking. As I read these verses in Mark, I realize that this is what Jesus would have said. Oh, he would have not cussed in church, but his language would have been harsh to this church leader.

These verses allow us to overhear Jesus blast the religious leaders who get so tied up in rules and regulations that they are missing the heart of the matter. Jesus quotes a little Bible to make his point when he says, "This people honors me with their lips, but their hearts are far from me; in vain do they worship me, teaching human precepts as doctrines."

Jesus has very little patience with the kind of attitude I encountered that night in that sanctuary. Jesus would have wanted to spend time with that young girl. He would have wanted to listen to her story. He would not have given a flip what she had on, and he would have been angry at the man who was in my face that night. Maybe there is nothing new under the sun. This is the same situation Jesus is addressing back then.

In these verses Jesus takes various rituals that the Pharisees have chosen as vital such as hand washing, and shows how empty rule keeping can be if the heart of the matter is not examined. Rules and guidelines are given to us in order to free us for living whole lives. Rules are not meant to enslave us, especially made-up versions of rules.

Jesus is concerned for the human condition. Rules, including the Ten Commandments, are God's way of trying to help us experience the fullness of life. If left alone, we do not do so well. God knows that sin will hurt us, so God points out sin. Rules help outline what sins are. It is not about keeping score. It is about life and balance and wholeness.

Jesus makes crystal clear that what is on the outside is not nearly as important as what is on the inside. Food regulations are of primary importance to the Jewish community of Jesus' day. Certain things would defile a person if eaten. Jesus opens the buffet and says, "Step right up." By the way I do not know what he is wearing when he says these words.

The adolescent who showed up in another sanctuary where I used to serve did not have on shorts. He had on multiple pieces of jewelry that filled various piercings on his nose, eyebrows and ears. He was arrayed with tattoos and his hair was in dreadlocks.

I was glad the aforementioned church leader from long ago was not there. The poor man's lip would have quivered into spasms and he probably would have had to pop a nitro tablet.

Again Jesus would have loved talking to this young man. Jesus would have looked past the piercings. Jesus' questions and comments would pierce into the young seeker's heart.

We are to do the same. Jesus knows that real evil and defilement comes from within. Church folks have the reputation for being the most judgmental people in the world. It is a bad reputation, much worse than the one that the girl whose legs were exposed that night in the sanctuary had. Such judgmental attitudes make those of us who get caught up in such attitudes become the truly naked and exposed ones. Jesus had X-ray vision long before the cartoon character who made the expression famous.

His kind of vision is what he is trying to share. It is a kind of vision that looks into the heart of the matter, not at people's legs.

MARK 7:24–37
THE SYROPHOENICIAN WOMAN/THE DEAF MAN OF DECAPOLIS

Mark closes this section of his writing with two more healing stories. His emphasis this time is not on the healings themselves but on who is healed. Mark has Jesus go to distinctly Gentile territories: Tyre and Sidon in the first case, and the Decapolis in the second.

If you look at a map, you will see that this route is like going around your elbow to get to your nose. Either Jesus is intentionally going places to prove his point about including Gentiles in the fold, or Mark is playing loosely with geography in order to make a succinct literary setting for his theological position. Mark does that kind of thing. This first-century writer is not concerned with details such as when Jesus does what or what his exact, literal, travel route is. Jesus' exact itinerary may never be known. Each Gospel writer places Jesus where he needs to be to make the point.

We must remember that the traditions which all the Gospel writers use are passed down and around a good deal before pen is put to papyri. Since Mark probably does not have at his disposal the exact details of Jesus' travels, he places them in the order that will fit his story line. This is okay. Do not panic. We do not have the film footage of Jesus' travels so it does not matter.

The fact that Jesus is described in these two stories as hopping from one side of Palestine to another should alert us not so much to Jesus not being a good travel planner, but more to the theological reality that something particular is going on here. That something is the early church's tension about who should be "in" and who should be "out."

Up until now, the question of who is in and who is out is not much of a question. You first have to be Jewish, and then there is a long list. The list of other rules and traditions is referred to in the previous section (see Mark 7:3–4). The "church" of Jesus' day had so many lists of rules, they were tripping over them.

Jesus does not exactly tear up these lists of rules, but he does say they are not primary. He also makes it clear that if the lists get in the way of saving lives they are to be set aside. The religious establishment's response to such a move is to find a way to set Jesus aside.

The first healing story in this section has bothered people ever since Mark put it to paper. The words of Jesus to this "alien" woman are harsh and almost mean-spirited. Whatever happened to "Fairest Lord Jesus"? Commentators speculate that Jesus may not actually have said these words but that they are put in his mouth to highlight the struggle that the early church was having over who to let in.

Have you ever used sarcasm to make a point? It seems to me that this is what Jesus is doing. I think one needs to be careful with sarcasm, but it can be a rhetorical device which gains the needed attention. Jesus could be asking a pointed question whose intent seems cruel in order to set up a foil against which he can make his point.

Why does Jesus have to be one-dimensional? Can we not allow him to use innuendo and sarcasm? This Jesus I serve was and is not cruel, but he does want to get his point across and he does turn over all sorts of established tables to get that point across.

Jesus looks at this woman who comes to beg for her daughter to be released from some kind of demon. She is not a card-carrying Jew, she has not paid her membership dues, she is not the right color, she smells, acts, and thinks funny. The list goes on. Mark simply states that she is from Syrophoenicia: an alien territory that Jesus is supposed to stay as far away from as possible if he wants to be a good Jewish boy much less if he is running for election as Messiah.

Jesus uses direct insult to gain everyone's attention, "You do not throw good bread to the dogs." That sounds as much like the Jesus that Mark has presented up until now as a Jesus who would advertise for the KKK. What is going on here?

Jesus is expecting a response. He wants a fight. He needs a fight to get on to the next level. He casts a line hoping for a bite.

Jesus needs this woman to offer a response of daring faith in order for him to move on to point number two in his sermon on "Just Who Can Be a Christian?" This "alien" mother comes through big time. Not only is her response on target, it is cunning.

I bet Jesus smiles when she takes the bait. When she says, "Yes Lord, but even the dogs under the table eat the children's crumbs," Jesus knows he is pulling in a big one. Jesus looks around to make sure everyone can hear this exchange and announces that the deed she requests has already been done because of her own words. The woman's child has already been healed.

Jesus knows that it is going to be tough going for outsiders to get in to this new kingdom he is bringing. The doors have been shut to the old kingdom for centuries. This woman's cunning and bold assertion is what he is looking for. She makes the moment. Jesus is saying, without actually having to say it, "See there, she has the kind of faith I am looking for. Forget who has a membership card and who does not. I am looking for a response. I am looking for faith, not membership cards."

If you are looking for an alternative explanation of this out-of-sorts Jesus then you can consider what some biblical scholars have come up with. What these theories amount to is that Jesus is simply having a bad day. Maybe he's tired when this woman confronts him. Can we allow Jesus to be tired? Anyway we may be back to the question of what kind of Jesus you believe in—one who is allowed to actually be tired and have a bad day, or one who would never go there. In this case, as one of my seminary professors used to say, "You pay your money and you take your choice."

The next healing happens a long way off in the region of Decapolis, another "alien territory." This time, a man is healed of his deafness and his speech impairment. Again he is an outsider not only because of who he is and where he lives but also because there is something different, or "wrong," about him physically. This renders him "unclean" according to another one of those religious lists.

Anne Lamott, a contemporary writer, tells in her book *Operating Instructions*[1] of five rules that her friend, Father Tom Weston, told her about. She says that these rules, which we learn as we grow up, are wrong and prevent spiritual growth.

These rules are: 1) "You must not have *any*thing wrong with you or anything different." 2) "If you do have something wrong with you, you must get over it as soon as possible." 3) "If you can't get over it, you must pretend that you have." 4) "If you can't pretend that you have, you shouldn't show up." 5) "If you are going to insist on showing up, you should at least have the decency to feel ashamed."

Jesus would object to these rules. Jesus is about healing and life. He doesn't want people to feel ashamed about who they are, or to be excluded for who they are. He wants them to show up and live. He cares about everybody, especially those who are in some way "different," or outsiders, and he wants the people who follow him to care about these people too.

The man who is deaf and has a speech impediment may represent all who are bound up in some way. When Jesus touches this man's mouth and ears, he reaches out to everyone who has ever needed to hear the word "Ephaphatha," which means "Be opened or unbound." That is all of us. Each person is bound up or closed down in some way. Sometimes we have subtle and creative ways of turning a deaf ear to the words that come to us describing our unique brokenness and naming our demons, and other times, we hear these words only too loudly, and cannot hear the words that speak of our own belovedness as children of God.

"Be opened" still rings down through the ages. Often our tongues need healing for they are capable of such great harm, or they need to be loosened to speak words of healing and reconciliation. Our ears may need touching because the wax build-up of prejudices and stubborn ideas can sometimes cause us to not hear words that have the potential to be life-giving.

We may also be blind to what Jesus is doing in these two healing stories for we have selective vision when it comes to what we see and what we choose not to see. Our field of vision makes "gentiles" out of those who do not fit into our categories of acceptance. Our vision needs Jesus' gentle touch and we need again to listen to those words first spoken to a resident alien who learns to listen to Jesus when he says, "Be opened."

ENDNOTES

1. Lamott, *Operating Instructions: A Journal of My Son's First Year,* 100.

Chapter Eight

MARK 8:1-21
MORE FOOD AND MORE QUESTIONS:
FEEDING THE FOUR THOUSAND AND THE YEAST
OF THE PHARISEES AND OF HEROD

What is the big deal about feeding four thousand when you have already fed five thousand? Ask the four thousand. Their stomachs are rumbling too.

Some commentators think this second feeding story is simply an older version of the first one. This story has fewer details in it but different numbers. The numbers could easily be symbolic. This time the number seven is primary which represents the Gentile nations. In the first feeding, which involved five thousand people, twelve was the primary number representing the twelve tribes of Israel.

Is Mark using material again to make his theological point? Is this like getting double prints at the photo shop and telling different stories about the same picture depending on who you are giving the photo to? Maybe.

The word Mark uses in this version of feeding the crowd is a word used also by Paul in referring to the sacrament of the Lord's Supper. It is the word from which we get the word "Eucharist," which means thanksgiving or blessing. By the time Mark's readers read this story, those who already know the story will inwardly smile as they remember the Lord's Table. Those who are hearing the story for the first time will be asking questions about "How does Jesus feed so many with such a small amount?" Such a question leads right into serving that person a small taste of bread and a sip of wine, while telling him or her of the abundant grace of the Lord Jesus.

The curtain is now raised on the next scene which finds Jesus in Dalmanutha. Ask me where Dalmanutha is. Ever heard of it? Do not worry, this is not *Bible Trivial Pursuits* and I am not trying to stump you.

No one knows where the place is. This may be a window through which we can peer, and see that biblical landscapes are sometimes beyond our horizons. Things have changed and so have places. Maybe it is one of those places that is called one thing but is another thing on the official map. You probably know of such places.

Wherever it is, the Pharisees show up and start harassing Jesus— again. This time they want "a sign from heaven." Jesus could again pull out the sarcasm stuff and respond to these wise guys with something like, "You know, the last time someone asked me to do that he looked a lot like the devil. Come to think of it, you guys sound a lot like him."

The text says that Jesus "sighed deeply in his spirit." We have all heard such sighs. Perhaps we have even sighed in such a way. It is the sigh when a parent picks up a child who has taken something from a store that is not theirs to take. Maybe it is a pastor's sigh when he or she deals with yet another picky fight between church members about some ridiculous issue when there is so much that needs doing for the kingdom.

If you have ever breathed such a sigh, you are in good company. Jesus looks at these religious leaders and says something like, "You guys . . . what is the deal with you guys? You are supposed to be the leaders of the religious community and you are demanding that I do one of those Elijah and Baal prophet tricks. Signs are up to God's timing, not yours. What is it with you guys?"

A lot can be said with one of those sighs of the spirit. What Jesus does say is pretty clear. After he finishes sighing he says, "No" and then the text says "he left them."

You can bet they do not sigh. They start running off at the mouth about who in the heck does he think he is talking like that to us? You say, "I don't see those words in the text." No, but actions speak louder than words, and later in the story it is apparent that mouths have been running, plans have been made, and the outline for making sure Jesus' sighs are quieted has been completed.

The scene now switches to Jesus with the disciples—you guessed it—in a boat again. Let's face it, a boat is one of the few places Jesus can be assured that he can talk alone with the disciples without someone either grabbing him, asking him yet another question, or demanding a sign from him.

Jesus more or less says, "Let's have a little pop quiz. What if I said, 'Beware the yeast of the Pharisees and of Herod, what would your response be?"

In Hebrew the reply of the disciples is something like, "Duh . . . Huh?" They start saying something about not having any bread in the boat so how could they be worrying about yeast. Jesus shakes his head from one side to the other and then places his face in his clasped hands.

Jesus is referring to the blatant misunderstanding the Pharisees possess about the meaning of his own message and life. Now he looks into the eyes of the very men he selects to convey the message and he wonders if they get it either.

Here again my translation would have him say back to them something like, "And you are the ones who are going to carry on what I am starting? When are you going to get with the program and realize that I am talking about something very different? What are those clumps of skin on the sides of your heads that you are supposed to use for listening and then hearing? Are your eyes glazed over with so many plans for the future that you do not see what is happening in the present?"

Jesus then switches from English and Biology to Math, "How many baskets of leftovers did you take up at the two feeding times? Yes, it was twelve and seven respectively. Get it?" The disciples look at each other and start counting on their fingers to see if this is some riddle that they have missed. Mark wants us to be sure to realize what a miracle it is that we have a church at all with the likes of these first disciples as the starting point.

What Mark is really doing by putting this story here is setting the stage for what is to come in a few verses when the turning point time comes at Caesarea Philippi. Peter will solve the riddle. The disciples will receive the 3-D glasses which will make alive what has been before them all along. They will have the chance to see who Jesus really is.

In light of this present story of the math lesson in the boat, Jesus will soon give them the chance for it all to add up. Stay tuned.

MARK 8:22–26
DOUBLE VISION: THE BLIND MAN OF BETHSAIDA

This story of the blind man whom Jesus has to touch twice in order to heal him is proof that Mark is a preacher. Obviously Mark is not saying that this man's blindness is such that Jesus needs somehow to hit him upside the head twice in order to clear his vision. Mark is clearly using this story to preach a sermon about the spiritual pilgrimage. Everything does not clear up at once. It does not for Mark's faith community and it does not for us.

A first encounter with Jesus is necessary but everything does not come into focus at once. Continued encounters with Jesus are needed in order for things to clear up. Okay, to be fair to first century understandings and healing, maybe Jesus does need to touch him twice. To me, the story has a wonderful human element to it.

I can just see Jesus touching the man's eyes and saying, "Now, how's that?"

The guy blinks a few times and responds, "I hate to say this, but when I used to have my sight a long time ago, people did not look like trees."

Jesus rubs his hands together and says, "Come here and let me try that again." This time the guy looks up at Jesus and sees not an oak but a smiling, very human and divine, Jesus. It is a great story and a good sermon.

MARK 8:27—9:1
THE REALLY BIG SHOW: PETER'S CONFESSION/THE WAY OF DISCIPLESHIP

Ed Sullivan's famous expression before his TV variety show might be a prelude statement for what now happens. It is time for the "really big show."

Up until now Jesus keeps his cards really close to his chest when it comes to who he is. In the Gospel of Mark, Jesus' title of preference for himself is the "Son of Man." He also hastens to quiet the demons who want to offer him his due as the "Son of God" or "Son of the Most High."

Jesus now takes the disciples to the villages which surround a notoriously Gentile city, Caesarea Philippi. If you look on a map, it is all downhill from here, so to speak. Jesus is now getting ready to head *down* to Jerusalem even though theologically he will be going *up* to Jerusalem. The *up* direction is has to do with a cross. The *down* direction has to do with a map. The *up* is of more concern to God and us. Anybody can buy a map. It takes a savior to buy a people gone astray.

It is time to show the disciples something. Jesus sets things up by asking what the talk is about him around town. Who are people saying that he is? The disciples offer some pretty good answers. Rumors have it that John the Baptist, who became a religious hero in a short period of time, has been resurrected and Jesus is none other than John revisited.

One could tell by this remark that a lot of people do not get out much because John and Jesus have, after all, been seen together. So much for that one.

One of the gang then says that some think that Jesus is none other than Elijah. This is not such a bad guess since Elijah is to show up on the scene just before God's fireworks are to go off at the beginning of a new age. In Jesus' day the present age is no fun with all the Roman occupation, religious red tape, and lots of poverty to go around. Elijah sounds pretty good. It sure is time for something to happen.

Then there is the multiple choice answer, "one of the prophets." Pay your money and take your choice. There has not been a true prophet for a long time. A prophet on the scene may indeed indicate that the new age of deliverance is just around the corner.

All of these answers would make an ordinary guy feel pretty good. Most of us would stick out our chests at such guesses. We are not dealing, however, with an ordinary guy.

Jesus is listening. The answers he hears prove that the disciples are listening—at least listening to the crowds. Now it is time to see if the disciples are really listening to Jesus.

Jesus then asks, "But what do you guys think?" I would like to think there is a dramatic pause. Perhaps they look at each other. Some of them, maybe even a number of them, either do not know what to say or have nothing to say. In Mark's presentation of these faithful but rather dense men, much is missing.

Peter stands up, or at least I like to think he stands up, and says what would have caused the duck to drop from the ceiling in the Groucho Marx program, *You Bet Your Life,* when a guest said the secret word. Peter blurts out, "You are the Messiah." He had spoken the secret words.

I wonder if Jesus sighs again, this time one of those sighs of relief rather than anguish. At least one of them gets the picture.

But, as is characteristic in the Gospel of Mark, Jesus quickly urges them to tell no one. As I mentioned earlier, there are plenty of expectations out there that Jesus is not planning on meeting when it comes to being Messiah. Things are going to be confusing enough without the people getting the wrong idea about Jesus' identity and plans.

Mark is far enough along in the story, however, that he allows Jesus to begin unveiling the secret of just what he is planning to do and be. He begins to teach the disciples about the suffering and rejection he will face at the hands of the authorities. As in another popular old TV show, *Let's Make a Deal*, Jesus picks curtain number three and out comes the prize.

As soon as Jesus brings out the prize, however, Peter strongly suggests that Jesus has chosen poorly and that he should take what is behind curtain number one. What Jesus chooses is not even a consolation prize; it is the "zonk" or booby prize—at least according to Peter.

Peter "rebukes" Jesus. This word "rebuke" is the same word Mark uses to exorcise a demon, so you get the idea that this is a pretty heated set of words that Peter uses. Peter did not sign up to go to Jerusalem and watch this guy he had given up so much for get himself killed. Peter is so intense and intent he does not even hear the word "resurrection" in the description of the prize.

Jesus then rebukes Peter with something like, "The devil you say!" Jesus has to regain control quickly before this brush fire becomes a forest fire. Jesus knows that his little band will not like what is behind curtain number three, but that is the prize.

Dying is never popular as a way to get things done, but that is the plan. Jesus basically tells Peter, "Look here buddy, remember who you are and who you are not. I am the leader. You are the follower. Do not get out ahead of me, get behind me. I know what I am doing. If I listen to you and your way of doing things, I might as well have stayed out there in the wilderness with Satan. He picked what was behind curtain number one too, you know. Now shut up and listen for a change."

Jesus really does say something like the above, but he says it succinctly. He simply says, in the old translation, "Get thee behind me, Satan." Jesus' temptations do not end out there in the wilderness with you know who. The temptation to do it another way is constantly before him. The other way bypasses the cross and is now championed by none other than the disciple whom Jesus picks to be the standard bearer for the cause. This needs to be nipped in the bud and quickly, before it gets out of hand.

Jesus has enough voices in his head luring him away from the hard way. He does not need voices on the outside suggesting alternate routes that lead away from Jerusalem.

The reason I am so sure about this is that in a former life I must have been Peter. His shadow somehow lives in me. I would have done the same thing that Peter does. In fact I have done the same thing many times when Jesus has led me down the path of self-denial and some form of ego death.

I have a healthy ego that knows how to defend itself against the suggestions of this one who is the Christ. Jesus' next words to the disciples about taking up crosses and losing one's life in order to save it still have the same sting now as they do to Peter back then. My self likes to be in control. I like to get out ahead of Jesus and plan the itinerary. The word "Lord" has a strange ring to me and my ego. How about you? Who is "Lord" in your life? Do you say, like me, "I like to be in charge, thank you very much"?

These few verses contain the core of Mark's Gospel and the core of the gospel in general. The way to salvation does go by Jerusalem, where the true disciples will have to give up control to a higher power. Wineskins burst, cloth gets pulled apart, and blood gets spilled.

I would have done it differently. I have discovered that many people sitting in church pews, if they are honest, do not really feel the need for someone to die for them in order for them to live. I have not polled those on the outside of the church who choose to stay away, but I have an idea that they find the story of "death in order to live" something foreign to the messages they consume in self help books.

Is it time for Jesus to tell me again to shut up and get in line behind him? Being a disciple of this Christ means following his way, not believing in his way, or writing books about his way, but following—not figuring out his way, or understanding his way—but following.

He knows our egos will put up a fight. He knows his way will not be easy. He knows sacrifice and servanthood will not be popular. He also knows it is the way.

Mark has Jesus close this section with some words that seem to entertain doubts as to whether we should risk following such a Messiah. Jesus says, "There are some standing here who will not taste death until they see that the kingdom of God has come with power."

Tradition has it that all the disciples but John meet a martyr's death, and soon. Is Jesus wrong? Is Mark wrong? Mark may think that Jesus is coming back before the disciples die. He probably wants him to come back and soon. Things are getting tough for Mark's faith community.

We know that Mark is not wrong even though he may think he is wrong on his deathbed. Seeing is not one of the disciples' strong suits, but all of them do manage to see the kingdom of God come with power before they get murdered. It finally does come to them. We know this because this little band do eventually pick up all of the qualities that Jesus describes as being those of a true disciple—along with a cross. (Except, of course, Judas who finally steps behind curtain number one and stays there until he comes out from behind it with some guards carrying clubs and swords.)

There is, therefore, a sense in which the disciples do not "taste death" before the kingdom of God comes. They all end up dying a death to self that allows them to meet their ends having seen the power of this new kingdom. Nothing could be a better goal for you and me than to hope for the same.

When we follow this Jesus we get to participate in the "coming of the kingdom" that he speaks of. Do you want to see the kingdom?—follow Jesus. You might not notice the kingdom because you are busy following Jesus, but others will see it. Trust me on this one—and if you can't trust me, trust Jesus.

Chapter Nine

MARK 9:2-13
THE TRANSFIGURATION AND THE QUESTION
ABOUT ELIJAH

If you have ever seen all the hype that goes on in and around the dressing room of a prize fighter just before a televised championship fight, you have a parallel to what happens to Jesus at the transfiguration. Former champions are present to give encouragement to the fighter who now has the focus on him. Close friends or handlers surround the fighter and offer words of encouragement and hope. It is a pep rally of enormous proportions before the anticipated contest begins.

Jesus is getting ready to step into the ring. Elijah and Moses stand behind him as Jesus robes up. Jesus' robe is that of a champion. It has the insignias of victory all over it. In big letters across the back of the robe in royal blue are two words, "My Son." Jesus fights under the sponsorship of none other than the God of the universe.

Elijah and Moses have been there before. They know what it means to step into the ring for God. Elijah remembers facing four hundred and fifty prophets of Baal (1 Kings 18:1–46). He knows what it means to realize that the odds are against victory. The betting was definitely on the side of that crowd of prophets. Odds of four hundred and fifty to one are too good to pass up. Elijah also remembers, however, who won that day. When the contest was over, there were four hundred and fifty knocked-out prophets and one man left standing in the ring. That man was in God's corner.

Moses on the other hand, has had a series of bouts (See Exodus 5-12). The biggest one was with the champion from Egypt. Moses needed all kinds of counterpunches to win that fight. Each round contained a plague. Pharaoh was a worthy contender. Though bloodied he went the distance. It was only in the last round that Moses delivered a knockout punch which had to do with taking the first born of Pharaoh to the mat for the count.

Moses also remembers how Pharaoh did not stay on the mat long and came out of the ring, like one of those TV boxers. Pharaoh and his legions chased Moses and his people all the way to the sea only to lose the rematch (Exodus 14). This time Pharaoh was suckered in by the "rope-a-dope." For those of you not familiar with this technique, made famous by Mohammed Ali, it is the technique of taking punches as if you are on the ropes only to come out blasting with a knockout punch just when your opponent thinks they got you ready for the kill. The result was Pharaoh watching his army drowned like rats on a sinking ship. Moses stood on the other side of the sea, raised his hands and his staff, and heard the bell of deliverance.

Now in this passage in Mark's Gospel, we see Moses and Elijah rubbing Jesus shoulders and getting him ready for the bout—what a sight! Peter, James, and John obviously do not know what to think or say. Let's face it, they are not doing too good with earthly matters. Now they are dealing with what biblical scholars call a "theophany."

Theophanies are when God makes an appearance, pulling back the veil for a moment, and the blinding light of heaven breaks forth. It is hard to look directly at the light, especially with human eyes.

These three disciples are squinting for all their worth to make sure they are seeing what they think they are seeing. All Peter can manage to get out is, "Do you want us to build three booths, one for each of you?" Peter uses the only language he has at his disposal. He learned in Sunday school about the Feast of Booths whereby booths are built to remind the faithful about the time when the people lived in tents in the wilderness.

No one can blame Peter for relying on his Sunday school faith. What would you have said? "Excuse me Moses, could I please have your autograph?"

Peter does not do so badly. Most preachers and commentators think that Peter wants to stay up on the mountain with all the hype and not go back down where the demons are waiting. Peter is high enough on the mountain to be breathing pure oxygen. He is getting high all right. He likes the feeling.

Jesus knows that they cannot stay there. After all, this is the hype before the fight. It is not the fight. Peter has already stated in the last chapter his opinion about going to Jerusalem for this contest. He thinks it is a very bad idea

Jesus is not going to let this inner circle of disciples breathe the mountain air too much longer. He has enough trouble getting them to follow him toward the cross without them getting high on religion. On the way down the mountain, Jesus tries to allow the disciples some time to decompress so that they will not get the bends. He starts telling them again about how he is going to suffer.

The disciples again revert back to Sunday school material and ask Jesus about the Elijah question. Even after the divine pep rally the disciples still do not get it. "Before the big day, Elijah will come, isn't that right Jesus?"

Jesus reminds them of John the Baptist. Elijah's picture is on the wall in the Sunday school room. "Think now," Jesus says. "John is as much Elijah as you are going to get, except for in heavenly visions."

Jesus tells these three disciples who are still high not to even try to tell anyone what just happened on the mountain until after his resurrection. They respond, "Resurrection? What resurrection?" Jesus looks over at them, realizing again that it is probably hopeless to try to explain. They will have to experience the resurrection before they understand or believe it.

The transfiguration is not for the disciples, anyway. It is for Jesus. Mark has Jesus say nothing in response to this mystical experience. Jesus just soaks it up. He will need all the divine soaking he can get.

Again Jesus hears a voice from the midst of the glimmer telling him, "This is my boy! Listen up!" Jesus will need to hear that reassurance a lot in the days ahead. He has been called a lot of things, such as crazy, son of the devil, Mary's kid, and he has been called down by his own disciples for thinking about such foolishness as going to Jerusalem and dying. To be called "my son" is very much needed by this one who will soon step into the ring, not only with the forces of evil, but with all those who thought they were "defenders of the faith", some of whom end up helping out the forces of evil without even knowing it.

The pep rally is over. There are demons in the valley, waiting. And just over the horizon Jesus can see the outline of an arena in Jerusalem where a ring waits. He will need this day of transfiguration.

MARK 9:14-29
THE BOY WHO COULD NOT BE HEALED
BY THE DISCIPLES

Jesus is trying his best to get the disciples ready. Like a good teacher who knows that he or she will not be able to follow the students around after class is over, Jesus attempts to transmit power to the disciples so that they can go on without him.

While Jesus is up on the mountain the other disciples are without him for a brief period of time and someone calls for a surprise exam. The remaining disciples are brought a boy whose symptoms greatly resemble what we would call epilepsy. Anyone who has ever struggled with epilepsy could tell you certain aspects of the way it feels are demon-like. The sufferer never knows when "it" will throw you around as it does the young boy in our story.

Yes, we know with our modern medical knowledge that this is not a demon, but the people in Mark's day do not. Remember we must allow the Scriptures to be what they are and not make them into what we would have them to be. Jesus deals with yet another "demon."

By the time Jesus and the "high and lifted up" disciples arrive on the scene, the scribes are arguing about something. Mark does not tell us exactly what the discussion is about, but given the track record of the religious leaders, they are probably pointing out that these disciples of Jesus have no business operating without a license. The scribes know about all the licensing requirements, and they know that the disciples have not even filled out the proper applications, much less passed the required tests.

These religious antagonists are probably relishing in the failure of the disciples to be able to heal the boy. It is a shame how religious types take great joy sometimes if their competition's spirituality, which is held suspect, does not come through with desired results. Organized religion seems to have a way of constant exclusion.

It is no wonder that the organized religion of the day does not have room for Jesus—in the same way that our organized religion often does not today. Jesus keeps looking below the surface like a carpenter looks for the reason the floor of a house is sagging. The scribes want to put carpet over the floor and keep on trucking. Jesus wants to rip up the boards and find out what is the cause. Jesus suspects spiritual termites.

Jesus asks what all the fuss is about and is told about the boy. Great detail is given about the boy's symptoms. Commentators tell us that this one story is probably a combination of two old versions of the same story. Mark likes to do this. Sometimes the material in each of the stories is too good to waste so Mark simply puts them together. The results seem for us to be a kind of overdoing or repetition. For Mark's original hearers it is probably like repeating the same line of a song for emphasis.

Jesus speaks with the father of the boy and says something that is still a challenge and maybe a threat to all of us who are Christians. Jesus says, "All things are possible to him who believes." This may be the most misused saying of Jesus. It is used to make countless people feel guilty for not having enough faith. A struggling believer is told that something would have happened if "you just had enough faith." Is this like some divine applause meter where if the level gets high enough something will happen? Many think this to be the case.

We need to read on. So many times Jesus' words are taken out of context. It is important to take Jesus at his word, but to take his word in its biblical context. Here again Jesus seems to be looking for a response. The father blurts out, "I believe, help my unbelief." We owe this dear father a great debt of gratitude. Does he not speak for so many of us?

We want to believe, but we struggle in our trusting. I told one of my young adult members who wondered why I asked him to attend a spiritual retreat that the reason I had asked him was not that he had great faith, but that he was "leaning in the right direction." This young man told me that other people would have been better candidates to attend the retreat, other people with more faith. I liked this young man's struggle to lean in the right direction even though there was much in the faith with which he had trouble.

Jesus likes those who lean in the right direction even though they have doubts. Doubts can make one lean away from faith and God. On the other hand our doubts can help us to honestly wrestle with the questions of our faith, and cause us to grow deeper in our spiritual development. As Anne Lamott pointed out in her book, *Plan B*, another piece of wisdom from her friend Father Tom, "the opposite of faith is not doubt, but certainty."

The father of this boy who could not be healed by the disciples is the patron saint for all of us who want so much to believe but who honestly have trouble trusting. Jesus honors this father's leaning in the right direction and cures the boy. I would like to commission a statue of this unnamed "saint of all who struggle to believe." I would ask the artist to make sure the statue was leaning just a bit.

Characteristically of Mark, the disciples who fail the test pull Jesus aside and moan and groan about why they could not heal the boy. "Did we not use the right words? Did we misname the demon? Did we not hold our hands right when we laid hands on him?"

Jesus simply responds, "This kind of rascal can only be driven out by prayer." I could go in all sorts of direction with this statement. I am sure many preachers have. Here again Jesus' words can be misused. How many have prayed for healing for themselves or someone they love only to not receive the healing for which they prayed? Did they not pray right? Did they not pray enough?

Prayer is full of mystery. Prayer is not manipulation of God. Prayer is trusting in God no matter what ends up happening. Prayer is relationship more than event. When we pray we are wanting to be with God. Yes, we can ask God for something, but prayer in the Christian tradition needs to remember the plea of this dear father. Prayer for the Christian disciple may need to end with "I believe. You know what I desire, so please help my unbelief if I do not get what I want."

Jesus, as usual, says it better; "Not my will, Father, but thine be done." Because faith is trust and not creedal statements, prayer always involves leaning into the mystery. There is power in prayer. Jesus says something along these lines in our story,

"You guys did not know what you were getting yourselves into. When you mess with the demons you must equip yourselves with prayer, wrap yourselves in prayer, bathe yourselves in prayer. Do not rely on your own resources alone. Do not even rely on my words alone. Pray, pray, and then pray some more. There is unseen power in prayer. You never really know what will happen but it for sure will not happen, when it comes to demons, without prayer. The demons always quake when they hear the name of the one to whom you pray."

Jesus knows that the disciples are going to have to learn what to do when he is not around in the flesh. He is attempting to teach them to pray to God. Soon they will be able to use his name in their prayers. In fact, because of the resurrection which they do not yet comprehend, they will be able to pray *to* him—just like we can now.

MARK 9:30-50
THE SECOND PREDICTION OF THE PASSION/THE COST
OF DISCIPLESHIP

How many of you who are parents remember saying to your children, "How many times do I have to say this?" Seventy times seven may come to mind, but that is another story.

Jesus again tells the disciples that he is going to be betrayed, or "delivered up" and killed. The disciples still do not understand. By the time Mark's readers see these words, the phrase "delivered up" will have the same ring to them as the phrase "saved" does now. The word "saved" has no particular import on its own. One can save money, save pickles, or be saved from having to do a chore.

When "saved" is planted in religious soil all sorts of things pop up. Many Christians have come to recognize it as *the* word to connote whether one is "really" a Christian. "Are you saved?" becomes the question for many Christians. I was once told that a good answer to this question is as follows,

"Are you saved?"

"Yes."

"When were you saved?"

"Two thousand years ago, on a cross."

All this brings me to my point. (I am not as succinct as Mark.) Jesus being delivered up takes on a technical theological meaning. Jesus' death comes to be understood in light of the sacrifice that had to be delivered up in order to save us all.

I am finding, as I alluded to earlier, that more and more people seem to be unable to relate to this need for sacrificial death. We must remember that all of this "delivered up" business is very Jewish. Jews at that time understood the need for sacrificial death in order for things to be made right. This sacrifice of blood was an important part of their tradition.

In response to Jesus' statement, Mark says that the disciples "did not understand this saying, and were afraid to ask." I find a number of Christians in the same boat. They hear about "Jesus dying for their sins," but words do not make much sense. Most of us are a long way from our Jewish roots. These "dying for us" phrases are ripped from their roots.

Paul writes, "Jesus Christ crucified; a stumbling block to the Jews and foolishness to the Greeks" (1 Corinthians 1:23). A good question to ask is, "Are you of Jewish or Greek persuasion when it comes to Jesus being delivered up for you?"

I think it is good for us to feel the tension. For too long, many have swallowed religious phrases like so many pills without knowing what it is they are taking. Examination of the original message, which by the way is what we are doing here in case you miss the point, shows us that from the very beginning people had trouble with Jesus being delivered up. A good dose of being bothered is part of the faith journey.

"Why does Jesus have to die?" is still a good and needed question. In way, it is the question that causes Mark to write his Gospel. Jesus could be viewed as a great martyr, a fine teacher, and a good example, but Mark's task is to show he is the savior of the world. It takes death to make him savior.

I, along with a lot of modern disciples, have trouble with this. If you are of the Jewish kind of persuasion, the source of your trouble is that you would rather have Jesus live than die a terrible death. The Jews do not want a crucified Messiah. They want a glorious, kick-the-Romans'-fannies, set-up-a-new-Israel-with-us-top-dogs type of Messiah.

If you are of the Greek kind of persuasion, your trouble begins in your head. The whole idea of the God of the universe becoming so weak as to end up getting crucified is just not logical. (*Star Trek* fans would call this line of argument "Spock Thinking.")

Here we have again the offense of the Gospel. Do not make the crucifixion of Jesus too religious, too quick. Allow it to be what it is. The first disciples have trouble with Jesus' crucifixion because they are on the front side of the Resurrection. Maybe we have trouble with the crucifixion today because we are on the back side of the Resurrection. We fail to see that it takes a God-awful death to bring life. We couch the crucifixion in terms of salvation so much that we lose its literal terror. We rush to resurrection and miss the reality of what it takes for God to get our attention.

Does God need Jesus to die? Mark thinks so. Mark buys into the plan. According to Mark, Jesus has to die to balance the scales. It is all God's doing. Jesus is doing his part. Those of us who are teethed on free will and choices have trouble with this. I believe we are supposed to have trouble with it. I have trouble with allowing my children to walk into painful situations, but I must allow them to do so if they are to mature and grow.

God did allow Jesus to die, but I fully believe that God did not want Jesus to die. What kind of God is that? God wants it to be another way. Jesus does have choices. Even in Mark's Gospel, with its almost predetermined plan, Jesus has choices. Jesus places himself in harm's way because he lives what he says.

The rest of chapter nine reveals what is behind Jesus' choice to die. First, Jesus catches the disciples arguing over who would be the greatest in the kingdom. If this isn't getting us right up next to modern-day discipleship reality, I do not know what is.

We who follow Jesus are continuing the disciples' argument. Are the Methodists better than the Baptists? Are my sermons better than the preacher's down the road? I could get real emotionally naked here. Do not worry or get excited, I am not going to strip off.

Suffice it to say, I understand this "wanting to be the greatest" thing. My ego loves to lead me around. Oh, I do it in the name of religion. I am like the funny saying, "I take pride in my humility." I need to observe what Jesus does next. He takes a child, puts her on his knee, and says, "This is what I mean." Children in Jesus' day are "least of all." In some places they still are.

Jesus now says, "This is my kind of greatness," and then he hugs the child. Jesus has in mind dependence. A human infant is the most dependent creature in all God's created universe. We are needier than any other animal. Look at babies in any other part of the animal kingdom and you will see that they are on their own much sooner than human infants.

"This is greatness," Jesus says. Jesus now turns his face toward Jerusalem and allows himself to be the kind of great he is picturing for the disciples. He becomes what looks like "helpless" in order to show real power. It is a risk for Jesus and it is a risk for us. This kind of willing vulnerability is not supposed to be wise or easy. This is what I mean when I ask you if you are of the Jewish or Greek persuasion. Stumbling blocks and foolishness are still important categories for us to keep in mind today, especially when we get into our contemporary discussions about who will be the greatest.

The disciple John now asks Jesus a question about competition. These guys really don't get it. It seems that the church down the street is attempting a new program that looks like it might work. They are using Jesus' name in their advertising. The disciples tear down the sign which is in front of the competition's church and tell them that this is not only a copyright infringement but that it is not kosher.

Jesus tells the disciples to go back, apologize, and put the sign back up. The disciples now probably get into another argument about just who will eat crow and go apologize. They are slow in understanding but good at arguing. Does this sound familiar?

Jesus tells them that he can use all the help he can get and hints that the disciples will need a lot of help in the future from all sorts of strange people. They need not be so selective so quickly. After all, that is what the religious leaders who are out to get Jesus are good at doing. "You don't want to be like them, do you?" Jesus asks. "If folks are not against us, they are for us."

Mark now has Jesus offer a series of sayings about making sure that new disciples, whom he calls "little ones" (in the faith), are taken care of. Jesus also strings together a series of "ifs" that definitely gain our attention. "If your eye causes you to sin, pluck it out—if your hand causes you to sin, cut it off."

Jesus, though very tolerant of all kinds of people, is setting up some quality control measures here for future discipleship. Let us not forget that although Jesus is open-minded and loving, he does expect extremely high moral standards from those who profess him to be "Christ."

Jesus uses exaggeration to make his point. Let's hope it is exaggeration, if not, most of the Christian community would be seriously missing body parts. We many times need to check out our impulses. Just because we are baptized does not mean all the dark impulses get washed away—I wish! Jesus knows better. He says, "Be vigilant. Monitor yourselves. I do expect quality when it comes to behavior."

Just to make sure we do not get caught up in the works-righteousness merry-go-round, Jesus ends these series of sayings by reminding the disciples that "Everyone will be salted with fire." Huh?

Jesus pulls back and puts all this morality and expectations in the context of his example and sacrifice. Salt was often used in the sacrifices of the day to represent purification. Jesus offers himself as a sacrifice for us. He knows we will fail in our morality. Morality is not what saves us; Jesus saves us.

Those of us who are still arguing about who is the greatest, or which one of us has the best morality score, need to again hear the old message. Our pride, even our religion, may think that Jesus dying for us is still a stumbling block or foolish. Jesus teaches and lives servanthood. Reach into your grown-up soul and find the child that is in there. Now, go sit on Jesus' knee and listen.

ENDNOTES

1. Lamott, *Plan B: Further Thoughts on Faith*, 256–57.

Chapter Ten

MARK 10:1-12
JESUS SAID WHAT? TEACHING ABOUT MARRIAGE AND DIVORCE

I have lost count of the number of marriages I have performed. If the marriages I have performed fit into the latest statistical data, fifty percent of them will end in divorce.

I have also lost track of the number of marriages I have performed for couples whose minister would not marry them because one of them was divorced. On one occasion I was allowed to marry a couple in their own church, but the pastor of that church would not do the wedding because the groom was divorced. Let me get this straight. You will allow me to perform the wedding in your church, but you will not do it? What is wrong with this picture?

We struggle with Jesus' words about marriage and divorce and sometimes we seem to lose the fight. Some people, such as the pastor I mentioned above, take Jesus very literally and end up asking more liberal preachers like me to do what would make them feel "unclean." Others just give up on Jesus and simply do not pay any attention to his seemingly harsh admonitions. One of these options sounds like pure legalism revisited and the other sounds like the secular world has won out.

In these verses, the Pharisees are trying again to trap Jesus. This time they are pinning him against the wall about divorce. Jesus does a little end-around maneuver. He begins by asking them what the Law of Moses states about the subject. Their response is that a man can give his wife a certificate of dismissal to divorce her. Jesus tells them that the reason for such a rule is that people are so hard hearted. The Mosaic Law is a protective measure designed to prevent men from divorcing their wives too casually, which was all too common. A woman of that time who is cast aside, having neither rights nor financial recourse, is in a precarious situation, economically and socially.

Then Jesus steps behind the Mosaic Law, and appeals to a higher law; he points to God's intentions for marriage. From the beginning of creation God set up a pattern for two people to be together, to support each other and care for each other. "The two shall become one flesh." A marriage relationship is supposed to be an equal partnership. A woman is supposed to be valued by a man as much as he values his own self, his own flesh; she is no longer to be considered mere property, as if she were a sheep or a goat.

Beginning with Moses' good intentions however, a whole maze of rules has sprung up. Rules that are intended to be protective and life-giving have become layered and complicated. The Pharisees have gotten so slaphappy with them that scribes and lawyers are needed to keep them straight. Jesus is not interested in all this legalism.

Jesus does his "new wine" thing. He explodes the law. Some liberals and free thinkers may be thinking that Jesus is getting ready to fling open the doors and make everything okay.

He does just the opposite however. He sets marriage up on a pedestal and dares the Pharisees to knock it off. He takes the disciples aside and tells them the now famous quote, which goes something like, "If a man divorces his wife, or a woman her husband, to marry another, he or she is committing adultery."

It is interesting that he specifically mentions women since at Jesus' time women cannot divorce their husbands. Women have no such rights. This probably relates more to the situation in Mark's faith community where women later come into such a right. Another interesting thing is that there are some Bible literalists, who may be divorced and remarried, who don't worry too much about Jesus' words in this particular passage but who are rather more interested in other passages which seem to indicate where others may be falling short.

Jesus seems not to be doing our modern world a favor here. What about second chances and forgiveness? What about marriages that should have never been? What about physical and emotional abuse? And, yes, what about those who simply mess up and do not work like they should on their relationships only to find the relationship dies?

In these verses in Mark, Jesus holds up marriage in very high regard. The not-so-good news for our "whatever" society is that Jesus will not back off about marriage. I mean, what do we expect? Do we really expect Jesus to start giving out loopholes? Rather, Jesus' intent is to support fidelity and monogamy, mutuality and respect; he does not want us to take our commitments lightly but to consider marriage as a sacred covenant.

At the same time however, we must remember the context for these words of Jesus. He is on the way to Jerusalem to make the supreme sacrifice for all of us who are wounded and who have failed in life. That includes every one of us.

Jesus reminds me of a sports coach whose expectations almost are beyond reality. The coach will be so intense that during practice many players wonder if they can make it. The expectations are not lowered for practice. A good coach makes practice even tougher than the game so that when the game comes we will be ready.

But what does a good coach do when we are injured or we lose? This is the good news that has "gospel" written all over it. I hope a good coach would not do what my high school football coach did after a game in which we got our back-ends kicked. He came into the locker room after the game and threw a clip board at me. He then called all of us names that I cannot print in a religious book.

Jesus, as a coach, wants us to take our game seriously, but he is also known to walk through the locker room and sit down with players after a losing match. He wants us to learn from our bruises and our mistakes. He does not just want us to forget and go on to the next game, nor does he want us to quit or change teams so quickly.

He does understand however, that sometimes we find ourselves in situations that are not life-giving to anyone involved. In such cases, marriage is not the place of companionship, protection and support that it is designed to be. God's intentions for marriage, and God's desire for the well-being of the individuals involved, are more important than legalism. God would not want us to be in a situation of danger, emotionally, mentally or physically.

My analogy needs shifting as we are getting ready to read the next section in Mark 10 about Jesus taking up the children in his arms and blessing them. In a similar passage in Luke (9:48), Jesus says to his disciples that the least among them is the greatest. Later in Mark, Jesus says that whoever wishes to become great must be a servant.

These words are useful as we consider what marriage can be and how we should relate in our relationships, and as we consider God's special care for the vulnerable among us.

Jesus becomes the trainer on his knees bandaging the wounded, wrapping hurting parts. Jesus is the healer. Those who come to him in faith, he does not turn away. Some of Jesus' ministers turn the wounded away. Jesus does not. We must remember that Jesus is on his way to Jerusalem to die for sinners; because of his wounds we may be made whole.

MARK 10:13-45

**ACTING LIKE CHILDREN OR ACTING CHILDISHLY?
RECEIVING THE KINGDOM AS CHILDREN/THE RICH MAN/
JAMES AND JOHN'S REQUEST**

I am not sure if Mark, when putting together this section with the three stories we are looking at here, has the same intent that I perceive him to have. In some cases, as I attempted to show earlier, we will never know Mark's intent, especially when it comes to how he arranges his material.

First Jesus tells the disciples, who are trying to shoo away a small group of children that are brought to him, that in order to enter the kingdom of God they must "receive it as a child." Next, a wealthy adult comes up to Jesus and tells him he wants to have his cake and eat it too—a complete misunderstanding of what it means to be a child. Finally James and John act in a childish rather than a childlike manner when they ask for the honor of sitting beside Jesus at a special place in the kingdom.

If I am right on this one, Jesus must be wondering by now if perhaps he needs to have a new draft in order to obtain a different team of disciples. He could put the present disciples on injured waivers and look for some first round draft picks from a new crop.

There is an ever-present backdrop to the stories of the disciples' misunderstanding of both Jesus' mission and his strong intention to go the way of suffering as he heads up to Jerusalem. The disciples are the blackboard on which Jesus writes lessons about discipleship.

Jesus has not long ago offered heavy words about marriage and divorce. Now, in his resistance to the disciples' attempt to keep the kids away, we have some balance. We see here more of a kinder, gentler Jesus.

The disciples may not be good at theological understanding but they are getting good at crowd control. They have had a lot of practice. This time, mothers are bringing their children to be blessed by this now famous healer and teacher. As mentioned earlier, children in Jesus' day need all the help they can get. They are among the most vulnerable in society; the mortality rate is high, poverty is the order of the day, and children's rights advocates are nowhere in sight.

If you look at the text closely, which I hope you are doing, you will see that the text does not say "mothers." It simply says, in the original language, "'They' were bringing children." I would like to think that it is the children's mothers that are bringing them. It makes for a better story. After all, women have almost no rights either and Jesus is getting ready to start a movement that will change all that. Since the text allows for interpretation, I say that the mothers are bringing them.

The disciples exercise their Secret Service role and attempt to send the children away. Jesus looks over and gives the disciples one of "those looks." The disciples don't always catch on to everything, but they are getting used to "those looks." The text says that "Jesus was indignant."

If you check your commentaries, you will notice that only in Mark's version of this story does Jesus become indignant, and only in Mark does Jesus bless the children. I like Mark—don't you? First of all, this is simply a window through which we see Jesus loving children in a very human manner. "Jesus loves the little children" begins here, not with a song. It is real in a world where children didn't have much going for them.

It is still true in our world today. It is children who suffer much of the brunt of societal injustice, deprivation and poverty. They are also often dismissed as nuisances, as young plants to be kept out back until they get big enough to bear fruit. We still need to hear Jesus' words about the primacy of children.

Jesus uses the example of the children to explain to hard-hearted disciples, "This is the way into the kingdom." I believe Jesus has some-thing in mind about a childlike sense of abandon. Young children often do not have to "let go" because they are still are big-hearted and coura-geous; they have not yet been bound up. Oh, they learn all sorts of ways to get uptight, but at first they are open, daring, and willing to try almost anything.

Jesus notices how "careful" and how full of cares his disciples are and presents to them the way of a child as a means of taking their first steps into the kingdom. The adult mind reasons away the kind of risks that Jesus proposes, the way of letting go to serve, the willingness to take a chance, all of these things.

As an example of such childlike risks, the story turns to the wealthy man who comes running up to Jesus, kind of like a child would, and asks him, "What must I do to inherit eternal life?" The disciples do not keep this guy away from Jesus, but after Jesus finishes speaking with this rich man, the disciples wish they had made him keep his distance.

Jesus asks the would-be disciple if he has been to Sunday school and recites a checklist of things the man should have learned there. The attentive inquirer replies that he has observed all of the Sunday school stuff since he was a youth. Better than some of us could say.

The next verse says, "Jesus, looking at him, loved him." In the Greek, this word "love" is "agape," which means that he is looking to the man's best interests. Jesus sees that the man is wrapped around his possessions. In other words, he doesn't own his possessions, his possessions own him. Jesus then lays on this man those words that echo down the years, but not down the halls of Wall Street, "Sell it all, brother, give it to the *Salvation Army*, and come join me on the journey."

The disciples, who are planning marketing strategy, cannot believe their ears. Just when they are about to figure out how to increase the membership rolls, Jesus comes out with this outrageous condition for joining up. Matthew, or at least Judas, figures that a wealthy man like this one could help with next year's budget. Now Jesus hits the prospective disciple in the solar plexus. Sure enough, after the man gets his breath back, he walks away. The original language says he is "astounded." So are we.

Is this normative for discipleship? No. Jesus does not ask everyone to do this. But if you are wrapped up in your possessions, as this man is, you'd better stay way back in the crowd. If you come up to Jesus and ask this same question, you might get the same answer. Remember, Jesus warns us that sometimes in order to follow him we will need childlike abandon. Be careful what you ask for.

The disciples, acting in character, pull Jesus aside and exclaim, "What did you say?"

Jesus responds with words that sound like fingernails scraping over a blackboard, "How hard it will be for those who have wealth to enter the kingdom of God."

Matthew and Judas are heard to whisper, "Oh great, there goes the budget."

Jesus looks at them, and guess how he responds—"Children, how hard it is to enter the kingdom of God." Jesus knows the disciples have a short memory.

This is followed by the famous "eye of a needle" passage. This passage is supposed to be bothersome and it is. I have many possessions. I am rich, especially by world standards. I have lived into the reality of how possessions and the reaching after security can lead one away from kingdom issues. It is not that possessions are all bad, but they really can get in the way of serving, loving, and giving. An overwhelming greed for possessions and a constant desire for more and better can lead to a lack of basic necessities for many others.

Jesus knows this all along. If we take the kingdom seriously we will "act like a child." This kind of paradoxical language is Jesus' kind of language. Jesus knows that grown-ups get wrapped up in making a living rather than making a life. Jesus' loving yet stern words to this rich man long ago are still words of warning today.

I work with people all the time in the local church who have learned to be "careful" when it comes to possessions. They are guarded and protective about what they have, yet they have said they want to follow Jesus. I have more than once remarked, "Well then, you'd better be even more careful. If you get too close to Jesus, he may ask you to get in touch with some childlike abandon when it comes to your hold on wealth."

I do not believe that Jesus asks many people to sell all they own in order to come and follow him, but I do believe that to be fully a part of this kingdom that he offers, we cannot be as tied to our possessions as most of us are—including me. To be asked to give ten percent of one's income to the church scares the heck out of many would-be disciples.

I have two things to say here—no I will not preach a full stewardship sermon right now, so you can keep on reading—1) Ten percent ain't "all" that you own. 2) You may need to sit on Jesus' knee like a child and let him bless you. Then go on and give what is right.

After the disciples respond to Jesus about his high expectations with the question, "Then who can be saved?" Jesus reminds them that what he is doing is a "God thing." The disciples have gotten so caught up in programming and organizing for the future they have forgotten that in order to do some of what Jesus expects there needs to be some help from God.

Peter jogs Jesus' memory that they have given up bunches in order to follow him. They know full well what it means to give up and follow. It is just that they wonder how many others will be willing to do the same. Is the movement going to end with these "dirty dozen"?

With this, Jesus seems to realize that his own "little ones" need some affirmation. They are children, after all. He looks into their eyes and tells them, "It will be okay." He acknowledges that they have given up much, and he tells them they will be rewarded for the risks they have taken. He blesses them as he has blessed the children earlier. Perhaps he senses that he has been hard on them.

Jesus the coach sits the team down and says, "I know it's been a tough game. You have practiced hard. Yes, you have lost some, but trust me you are going to be big winners in the end. Hang in there. It is all going to be worth it."

They will need to remember this pep talk. It is going to be rough, and then it is going to get rougher, before it gets better.

Just when we think the disciples might finally be getting the picture, Mark brings us back down to earth with James and John's response to Jesus, when Jesus, for the third time, announces his upcoming suffering. Jesus has taken the disciples aside as they are walking to Jerusalem and has told them even more vividly that he will be condemned to death and killed in a brutal manner.

And what is the response to this passion-filled statement? James and John's first thought is to ask Jesus if they can be first and second in line when it comes time to receive the awards. They finally get the *child* thing, but rather than acting childlike they end up being childish. Jesus gives them the "no pain, no gain speech," about his future path through suffering, but they just don't get it. Childishly, they bob up and down and say, "Oh we can join you in that. We can do that."

Like a loving parent, Jesus gazes at them, and says, "You have no idea what you are asking for." Against the backdrop of the other disciples, who are pushing James and John around like a bunch of teenagers roughhousing, Jesus tries to bring order to his not-so-orderly band.

He reminds them again that he is trying to start something new. They need to quit using old paradigms. The world "out there" has a different way of life that Jesus has come to challenge. The disciples keep trying to take the old and bend it a bit to make something new. Jesus is breaking in the new, not bending the old.

Jesus tells James and John, "it is not mine" to give out first place prizes in the kingdom. He reminds them about the superior officer that he reports to. He then goes on to plead with them to listen and look at his example. He is their leader, but he is a servant. Is that so hard to get? He tells them that the "Son of Man came not to be served but to serve." Jesus is transforming people's understanding of who and what the "Son of Man," and the "Messiah" would be. Glory is going to come in a different way than everyone, including the disciples, are expecting.

Jesus closes this time together with his disciples with the powerful image of "giving his life as a ransom for many." The word used for "ransom" means "to pay the price of release for a captive." Some commentators think that this is the early church putting theological meaning into Jesus words. This *is* the way the early church comes to understand the death of Jesus. Whether Jesus explicitly lays it all out here is debatable. Maybe it is not debatable to you.

Whatever the case, one of the ways of understanding Jesus' death is as a ransom. However we may understand Jesus' death, perhaps the relevant question for us is, "Do you feel ransomed?" Do you have a sense of having been delivered from something? Theologically speaking, Jesus has paid a price for us. Do you believe that or is it just lofty-sounding religious language? As I mentioned earlier, it seems to me a lot of people both inside and outside the church are saying in responses to this "ransom" language, "I do not need you to do that for me."

Jesus does it anyway. As the record shows in Mark, Jesus is used to people not paying attention or believing. God acts in spite of our predispositions. As I often say in various liturgies, "Thanks be to God."

MARK 10:46–52
WHO IS REALLY BLIND?
THE HEALING OF BLIND BARTIMAEUS

Mark is a master at placing events so that words and actions come together to make living parables. Jesus lectures the disciples again about what discipleship really means. It does not mean asking for the number one and number two spots in the kingdom as James and John have just done. It means being willing to be last, being willing to serve rather than be served, and being willing to die in order to live.

Mark now relates the story of a man who is blind. He has enough faith to call out to Jesus and to respond with determination to Jesus' voice. Bartimaeus throws off his cloak, springs up and runs to Jesus. Even though the crowd around him, and maybe even the disciples, try to quiet Bartimaeus, he will not be still. He responds quickly to Jesus' call.

Mark obviously places this story here to highlight true sight, which is based on faith, in contrast to the disciples' blindness. If you do not think that Mark is doing this, just look at the question that Jesus asks of Bartimaeus, "What do you want me to do for you?" This is the same question that Jesus asks of James and John a few verses earlier. James and John do not ask for vision based on faith. They ask for positions of honor in the new administration.

I wonder, when Jesus asks this blind beggar the same question he had just asked James and John, if Jesus does not cut one of "those looks" their way. How much is it going to take for his disciples to see?

Jesus almost routinely cures Bartimaeus. The emphasis, however, appears to be on the way that Jesus calls him. Jesus offers this newly-sighted man the opportunity to go on his way but Bartimaeus chooses to follow Jesus.

This story is like a drum roll before the curtain comes up on the main act. Someone who is blind is given their sight in preparation for the entrance into Jerusalem where so many will have the opportunity to see for themselves what God is doing, but will not understand. Bartimaeus, though blind, is able to recognize who Jesus is. He is almost like a blind prophet. He twice calls Jesus, "Son of David" and we will soon hear echoes of his words.

We sometimes say that from the mouth of babes comes truth that we cannot gain from lofty, adult ways. Perhaps vision sometimes comes from those who are "blind." I sometimes learn gospel lessons from people who claim not to be disciples. God is at work outside the church as well as inside. We need to keep our eyes open. Sometimes our religious blinders keep us from seeing and learning lessons. The disciples discover this over and over again.

Chapter Eleven

MARK 11:1-11
THE BEGINNING OF THE END: THE ENTRY
INTO JERUSALEM

It is now time for the beginning of the end. The healings are over. The primaries are completed. It is time for the election.

Jesus has presented his teachings and offered a taste of the new kingdom to the outlying regions. It is now time to go to Jerusalem.

In basketball terminology, it is the *Final Four*. Everything points to these few days and everything depends on what happens these next few days.

The pressure is on, but you would not know it to look at the scene on the road into Jerusalem. Jesus has sent the disciples on an errand. This time, instead of picking up a few groceries, they are to bring back a colt that has never been sat upon. Jesus has read his Bible. He knows that the deliverer of David's people is to come into the sacred city in a specific way. This expectation he will meet. Many others he will not meet.

The disciples find the colt. Jesus has either prearranged such a situation or he knows that there will be some willing soul in the village who is hungry to provide a means of deliverance for the people, even if it just means lending his colt.

The Mount of Olives looks down on Jerusalem. If you have never been there, go—if you are able. Just standing on the Mount of Olives and looking down on this sacred city whose history is rich with blood and meaning is worth the trip.

Jesus knows that the Mount of Olives has deep significance to the people who hope for the coming of God's kingdom. Something big is supposed to happen on the Mount of Olives just before God shows up. Jesus is not going to play the part according to the script that so many have written in their hopes and dreams, but he is going to do just enough to make sure that people know this is God's doing. He knows they will later have to sort it out for themselves.

The disciples sense that what they have been thinking all along *ought* to happen is finally *going* to happen. Their candidate, the one they have given up so much for, is going to be heralded as "the man for our times."

The disciples throw their cloaks on the colt, which is a first-century equivalent of a balloon release at a political convention. They could just hand out the printed placards reading, "Jesus–The Man We've All Been Waiting For." It is parade time.

Sure, this is not a Mercedes convertible that their man is riding in but who cares? His entrance comes in something more like a VW convertible, but whatever, it is a parade. The disciples are more than ready for some hoopla after all Jesus' talk about being humble, quiet, and servant-like. The disciples are not so much into the humble scene.

They are right in the middle of the hosannas. In fact they are lifting their hands to encourage even more of the crowd to join in. This time they give up on crowd control. Heck, they have not been doing such a good job anyway. Now they let the crowds pour in around Jesus. It is their version of "Jesus, Jesus, he's our man. If he can't do it nobody can."

Of course such a cry echoes over the walls into the waiting ears of the religious leaders. They are preparing a response to such a cry. That is why this gala event is the beginning of the end.

Remember that the word "Hosanna!" means "For heaven's sake, save us!" It is a plea for help. These excited people are, after all, desperate people whose hopes can easily be dashed and whose joy can turn to anger if they are disappointed yet again by someone who makes promises that they cannot keep.

Jesus has not made some of the promises that this crowd thinks he has made. Some of the people in the crowd on this parade day are filling in the blanks on the form which state, "What do you want your Messiah to be?" Many of their answers are descriptions of someone whom Jesus has no intention of becoming, but they do not know that—yet.

This "filling in the blank" kind of thing is a familiar pattern in religious practice. I see people do it all the time. We formulate what we want and need God to be, and then we mail in our form. Many of us are disappointed when God does not come through being who and what we want God to be. Trouble is, God never agreed to "be" according to our standards. That is what makes God, God. God is. We have to deal with what God is.

Jesus fully understands this. People who line up along the way to Jerusalem that day probably do not. They are tired of waiting on God. They want action and they want it powerful and quick. Jesus seems to fit the bill. He attracts big crowds. He has majestic powers. He is unpopular with the religious authorities. It sounds like a done deal. Some of the people are willing to make Jesus Messiah even if he does not want to be their kind of Messiah. It is time. The waiting has been too long.

Jesus takes all this in. In Mark's Gospel he says nothing to the crowd. He simply goes to the Temple, "looks around at everything" and then leaves.

He will wait to turn over tables. He will wait to say anything. He simply goes to the Temple. Maybe Jesus just needs to take a look at what he is getting ready to challenge, and challenge big time. Or maybe he wants to stand there a moment, and close his eyes, and whisper a word to his Father. Maybe he says, "Oh Dad, this is your place, but I wonder if you any longer feel at home here?"

All Mark says is that "it was late" and that Jesus went to rest with his disciples. It is late all right. It is later than any of them imagine it to be, except Jesus. He knows exactly what time it is. He knows that the time is at hand.

MARK 11:12-26
CURSING AND CLEANSING: CURSING THE FIG TREE AND CLEANSING THE TEMPLE

Maybe Jesus is having a bad day. Will we allow Jesus to have a bad day? Would Jesus ever kick the cat after a rough day at the office? I know some of you cannot possibly imagine Jesus doing any of the above. The mystery of the incarnation is just that, a mystery. How can divinity contain humanity and vice versa?

The reason I mention this "bad day" stuff is that what happens next seems strange. Jesus drops by the drive-thru for breakfast. They are out of eggs. Jesus loves scrambled egg sandwiches and for heaven's sake—pardon the expression (again)—this is a restaurant. How can they possibly be out of eggs?

The problem is that breakfast time ends at 10:30 and it is 11:00. Being out of eggs is understandable. Jesus gets upset and puts a sign out in front of the restaurant saying, "May You Never Serve Breakfast Again!"

In a nutshell, this is what Jesus does. He walks up to a fig tree. Mark clearly states that Jesus is hungry. That may be surprising to some people. Jesus does get hungry. He probably has favorite foods, which means he has some he does not like. I would like to think that Jesus does not like liver. In fact I wish Jesus would write his father and have liver taken off everyone's menu forever, but that is another story. (I hate liver, in case you missed the point.)

My point is that Jesus is human. What we have trouble with is how human to allow him to be. In this story he is real human. He walks up to this fig tree, and it seems his hunger gets the best of him. He wants figs and he wants one now. The problem is that it is not fig season. The tree has plenty of leaves on it and maybe lots of blooms, but no figs. It is not time for figs.

Jesus steps back and says loud enough for the disciples to hear, "May no one ever eat figs from you again." Mark, with all his literary techniques and theological posturing simply says, "And his disciples heard it."

Remember that Mark does not waste words. Mark must want us to know that the disciples hear what Jesus says. Maybe Peter says to John, "We'd better go back to Bethany if the day is going to start this way." Matthew may whisper to James, "I guess we'd better shape up and start putting out even if we do not think we are ready! If he can do such things to this poor tree, what is he going to do to us if we do not shape up?"

Our biblical scholar friends tell us that this strange story may just have been an illustrative story that Jesus tells his disciples, but somehow it has become a story in which Jesus and the tree are characters. Jesus, up until this point in our story, does not go around cursing things that do not go his way. Even allowing for Jesus' humanity, it is rather strange for him to destroy a living thing rather than restore it.

The story of Jesus and the fig tree appears on either side of his description of Jesus' cleansing of the Temple. This sandwiching technique is one of Mark's literary styles. It may be that Mark wants us to see the tree as a symbol of the Temple, and that Jesus' curse was an indictment of its practices. The fig tree was considered symbolic at that time.

In the second part of the story, as Jesus and the disciples are passing by the next morning, Peter sees the fig tree that is now "withered away to its roots." (And you thought *Round Up* was bad.) Jesus uses the zapped tree as an excuse to preach a mini-sermon on faith and prayer. This sermon reminds me of some of the sermons that I have heard where what is said does not quite match the text that was used.

Standing beside the unfortunate tree, Jesus says, "Have faith in God." Then he starts talking about mountains. I like what the scholars say here. Mark is pulling together a lot of different elements from separate sources. Mark uses what he has and puts it together according to his own theological plan.

Mark may also be making the point that faith is something that needs to happen now no matter what the season. There is no waiting. In Mark's time the eschatological fever is running high. (*Eschatology* is a big word that means *the end times*. I just wanted to make sure you know I went to school . . . for a long time.) Many of Mark's readers think that Jesus is coming back "any day now." The time for faith is now, no waiting. Israel has had many seasons that it could have produced, and has not.

Jesus talks about the power of faith to move mountains and the power of prayer to affect all of life. With a withered fig tree in the background, one wonders just where Jesus is going with this. I think we have a context problem. Mark may have understood the context. I am not sure we do.

Having said all of this, Jesus' words about prayer and faith do sound like Jesus. He tells the disciples and those of us who overhear Jesus, that prayer has power, mysterious power. When real faith is mixed in with prayer, marvelous things can happen. Jesus does not let us get too "high and lifted up" about prayer, however, for he also makes a point of linking the human dimension to the divine. He states that if we want forgiveness from God, it is connected to our willingness to forgive those who have wronged us. We often forget this connection. Could it be that when we do forget, we become like fig trees with no figs. Okay, I tried to make sense of all of this. Did I succeed?

Now let us return to the focus of this chapter, the "cleansing of the Temple."

When Jesus goes to the Temple he "cleans house." He quotes Scripture as his reference point and tells the very unhappy money changers and dove sellers that the Temple is supposed to be a "house of prayer for all the nations," but that they have turned it into "a den of robbers." He brings the original purpose of the Temple to the forefront, as if this is the one thing that matters, that it be a "house of prayer for all the nations," It may be that he is also making a statement that the whole sacrificial system is becoming obsolete.

Needless to say, Jesus loses the little support he has from the money changer caucus and the pigeon seller political action committee. His disciples stand by thinking, "This is no way to win an election." If those same disciples look up to the balcony they will see the scribes and the chief priests rubbing their beards and pointing their fingers.

These religious leaders are probably also smiling because this is the very best thing that could happen to fit their plan to get rid of this religious upstart from Galilee. Mark says that the religious leaders "feared him because the whole crowd was spellbound by his teaching." These same religious leaders know that election time is at hand and they are the ones who will stay in power, not this new guy. Fearing Jesus' candidacy they decide not to take a chance on a popular vote. It is time for another kind of cleansing. For the religious leaders the best way to really cleanse the temple is to sweep Jesus out of the picture.

This day the religious leaders hold their own election. The vote is in. Jesus is out. Now the only decision that is left for them to make is how and when to cleanse Jesus from the scene.

MARK 11:27–33
THE QUESTION ABOUT AUTHORITY

For those of you who used to watch *Perry Mason* or who now watch TV courtroom dramas, Jesus' exchange with the chief priests, scribes, and elders should sound familiar. In such courtroom dramas there are twists and turns with the usual results being that one particular set of questions lead to a sudden revelation or confession.

In this drama, the Sanhedrin, the council of judges, confronts Jesus. These guys are not officially in session but the listing by Mark of this group reveals the same constituency as the high court of the Temple. This is the group of individuals that will soon sign Jesus' death warrant.

You might think these particular religious leaders would learn by now that it is hard to trick Jesus into answering their way, but they desire to have some more evidence before they do what they are going to do anyway. They have not had a trial, but the verdict is determined. They are just trying to get some material that will look good for the newspaper.

Mark will now show a series of controversies between Jesus and this same group. The antagonists try to trip Jesus up by asking him just where he gets his authority to do "these things." It is a wonder Jesus does not say, "What things?" It might be embarrassing for the scribes and elders to have to rehearse all the marvels that Jesus has done. They would not much want to hear about all the healings and demon exorcisms. The "things" about which they are asking are signs of a new kingdom. It is a shame that Jesus does not now list them.

Jesus refuses to answer their question until they first answer a question that he has for them. In other words, he takes authority, even in this moment. Jesus asks them if the baptism of John was from heaven or of human origin. The questioners, you can bet, are irritated, but they are the ones who started it so they have to say something. Besides, they can probably overhear some in the crowd snickering. They know they have been "had."

They huddle and quickly discuss their options. Jesus has them penned in. If they answer one way, the people will start asking their own questions. If they answer the other way, it makes the religious establishment look foolish.

What the religious leaders really do is take the fifth; they refuse to answer on the grounds that they know they are in trouble. What they really want to say is, "Wait a minute. Who is on trial here anyway?" But they cannot say that because Jesus is not yet supposed to be on trial, even though he is.

They know they have lost round one so they retreat to fight another day. Since this is Mark and the words and time are short, maybe it would be better phrased "to fight another hour." Jesus smiles and tells them if they will not answer his question then neither will he answer their question. This is cute, but deadly.

Jesus' little question is loaded, if looked at closely. Not only is he snagging the leaders in their own trap, he is also reminding all who are listening that John came preaching repentance, especially to the religious establishment. The religious leaders hate to be reminded of their dirty laundry—don't you? Jesus has definitely gone from preaching to meddling, but then he has been doing that for a long time.

The difference now is that Jesus is in their territory. The sounds that can be heard as the parade ends are the gates of Jerusalem closing behind Jesus like the door of a cell. This is not literally true, for Jesus comes and goes in these next few days, but it is figuratively true because the religious leaders see him stepping into their snare. What they do not know is that Jesus knows exactly what is happening and what he is doing. They are the ones "who know not what they do."

Chapter Twelve

MARK 12:1-12
THE PARABLE OF THE WICKED TENANTS

Jesus now goes back to storytelling, except this time the stakes are higher and the parable is about him. As I said earlier in this book, everybody likes a good story. The Pharisees listening to this particular story would take exception to my generalization.

Jesus tells a tale about a vineyard owner whose tenants do a number on him. It seems that the owner keeps sending representatives to collect his share of the produce from the tenants. The tenants keep roughing up the collectors and sending them home. The infirmary is getting full of wounded collectors.

Finally one collector returns to the owner in a body bag. You would think this would stop the sending of collectors but it seems the owner is intent on getting his fruit from the vineyard. Finally after the body bags start piling up, the owner sends his "only beloved son" to do the dirty work. One might question the wisdom of the owner, but this is a parable after all.

The only son shows up on the scene with a truckload of empty baskets ready to be filled. The fruit is ripe for the picking, but instead, the wicked tenants pick on the son, beat him, and kill him. They figure the old coot who owns the vineyard must be mighty stupid and senile. If they kill the only heir to the place then they can keep the vineyard for themselves.

The story is obviously about the Pharisees and their plot to do in Jesus. Jesus may as well show slides and use a pointer to detail the plot. Needless to say, the Pharisees are ready to make this a self-fulfilling prophecy and string Jesus up right then and there, but they notice that the crowd seems to be rather enjoying the story Jesus tells at their expense.

Mark simply states when they realize that Jesus is telling the parable against them, the Pharisees "left him and went away." The crowd more or less says, "Don't leave mad, just leave." The Pharisees are not happy campers. Jesus pours salt on a sore.

My imagination tells me that some of the disciples probably pull Jesus off to the side and tell him that he'd better back off. I can just hear Peter say, "Did you see the look on their faces, Lord? You don't have to make this so obvious, do you?"

Jesus' answer is, "Yes." Of course what is really happening is that Mark is putting this all together to make the scene obvious. Mark wants his readers to fully see from this parable that Jesus and God know exactly what is going on.

If this is round two, you can bet that the Pharisees are getting tired of being publicly browbeaten by Jesus in front of the crowds. Getting rid of Jesus by pulling off something behind the scene is looking better all the time to these frustrated religious leaders. The public stuff is not working. Plan B is set in motion, but first there are some last minute skirmishes left to be fought.

MARK 12:13-17
PAYING TAXES TO CAESAR

We have all heard the expression "to flip a coin." It is one method of deciding something one way or another. Jesus now has a coin flipped in his direction. The coin comes with yet another question intended to snare Jesus in controversy.

Now, along with the Pharisees, we have the Herodians getting in on the act. The gang that is attempting to do Jesus in is growing. It should not be surprising that a political party with Herod's name attached to it now appears on the scene. We do not know much about the Herodians except that Mark wants us to know that Herod has a stake in how the coin toss goes. Herod serves at the pleasure of the government. The government imposes the tax. The connection here is obvious.

The people who make up the crowd hate this tax, which must be paid with coins just like the one that is tossed Jesus' way. On the coin is the image of Caesar, the very one who is responsible for the people's bondage. The religious leaders are testing the waters to see if Jesus will give the crowd what many of them want: political and economic revolt.

It will help the Sanhedrin's cause if they can clearly show that Jesus is inciting the crowds to revolt against the government. It would not hurt their feelings if Rome would take care of this troublemaker. Herod and the religious leaders are still smarting from the unrest that came from the beheading of John the Baptist. John was popular with the people. The religious authorities, while despising many of the common folks, need them not to cause trouble. The sight of Jesus being hauled off to jail by the civil authorities would be a real boon for the scribes, elders, and Pharisees.

Jesus again dances around their trap. After asking them whose image appears on the coin, he gives the famous answer, "Render to Caesar the things that are Caesar's and to God the things that are God's."

Those who ask the question ask if paying taxes to Caesar is lawful. Everybody listening that day knows it is lawful. The question is whether or not in the eyes of this new religious leader the law is right. The Romans have brought law and order to this tumultuous land but at a high price.

Jesus takes this coin from a Pharisee, who technically is not supposed to be carrying around such an "unclean" coin. He gives his antagonists one of "those looks" and says only one sentence. He does not answer their question. They should be used to that by now. When are these guys going to give up? The truth is that they are never going to give up.

The unasked question in Jesus' look, which speaks louder than his words, is, "And do you religious leaders want to tell everybody here just what belongs to God? . . . Huh, do you?" Jesus reminds them of who they are supposed to be. I am sure the religious leaders appreciate that.

Jesus does not get us off the hook when it comes to taxes. Sorry. He implies that a government is due its share. But then there is this God stuff. Remember who is talking. This representative who comes straight from God, and who is getting ready to give it all, simply says, "Render to God what is God's."

Mark's readers will see the big picture. Everything is under God. Rome will not recognize this. Rome does not care. The people who follow Jesus have to care. Being a citizen has its place as a follower of Jesus, but Jesus places citizenship in his new kingdom as primary.

The way this all works out is that if kingdom citizenship conflicts in an ultimate way with country citizenship, the Christian must wrestle with priorities. This has been the case ever since Jesus spoke his words.

There are hard decisions that Christians must make. Jesus does not make the choice easy. He does lay the groundwork for there to be times when choices will have to be made between the citizenship in the kingdom of God and citizenship in those kingdoms that are under God's rule.

In the present moment, however, Mark simply tells us that the religious leaders "are utterly amazed" at his answer. They might be amazed but they are not ready to stop asking questions of him in order to trip him up.

MARK 12:18-27

THE SADDUCEES AND THE RESURRECTION

Mark wants his readers to know that attempts to discredit Jesus are coming from across the religious establishment. He now needs to make sure the Sadducees get in on the act. The Sadducees are more political and priestly than the Pharisees.

They have something to lose if Jesus wins because they are "biblical fundamentalists." The Sadducees believe only in what is written in the books of Moses (our first five books of the Bible); they refuse to acknowledge any of the later writings. There is nothing about a resurrection from the dead in the books of Moses, therefore "it just ain't so because it is not in the Bible!"

Jesus knows that these guys do not believe in the resurrection. They themselves know they do not believe in the resurrection, so the convoluted question—based on some laws within the books of Moses—that they present to Jesus, about seven brothers who all die like dominoes falling and end up marrying the same poor woman, is even more ridiculous than it sounds. It is like an atheist asking a Baptist to explain exactly what God looks like. Why should the atheist care?

Their inquiry also reminds me of the absurd old question that asks whether God is powerful enough to create a rock so heavy that God couldn't lift it.

The Sadducees, of course, are trying to make Jesus look stupid. They should check things out first with their Pharisee friends about the track record when it comes to making Jesus look foolish. The Sadducees would discover left-over pieces of egg on the Pharisees' faces.

Jesus points out to the Sadducees that, first of all, they do not really understand the Bible from which they quote. I am sure that goes over real well. Then he says they are like the one asking the question about the heavy rock. They misunderstand the nature of God's power.

They are misusing Scripture for their own purposes and underestimating God's power to give life. They are trying to understand heavenly realities with earthly minds. What is left unsaid but which Mark hopes his readers will pick up is that these "old age thinkers" are stuck in the past and cannot understand the "new kingdom" person who is talking to them.

Jesus' answer may not make some of us very happy. He tells them, for us to overhear, that there is no marriage in heaven. Come to think of it, that may come as a relief to some people. For those of us who cherish the companionship of a life-long mate, Jesus' words may cause some discomfort. We need to remember that we are in the same boat as the Sadducees when it comes to understanding heavenly realities.

Heaven is simply bigger than the human mind can comprehend, but that does not stop us from trying. We want to know. We want to know that we will recognize each other and that relationships that we cherish will continue beyond death.

We cannot imagine something better than the joys we presently have. For Jesus to tell us that what is so important here will not be important in heaven is not enough. Well, we are going to have to trust Jesus on this one. God's love is bigger than all our loves here in our time.

By the way, I still want to know my mom and grandmother are waiting on me in heaven. I want to know that my wife will still be my wife. Jesus and God know that I want these things. I am sure they have discussed it. Heaven is somehow the fullness of all that can be. God loves us and wants completeness for us. So even though marriage may not be as important in heaven as it is here, maybe because it is part of who we are, God will somehow give us what is important over and above the need to know each other.

Does that make sense? If it does not, just rack it up to "We cannot always understand heavenly realities."

Jesus ends his discussion with the Sadducees by quoting some Scripture to these biblical sticklers. I am not sure that Jesus is trying to be sarcastic in doing this, but remember he is capable of using sarcasm to make his point.

In response to their question about resurrection, Jesus refers them to one of the foundational stories in the books of Moses, which can be found in Exodus 3. When God calls to Moses out of the blazing bush, God announces, "I am the God of Abraham, Isaac, and Jacob." All of these heroes' names had already appeared in the obituaries at the time of Moses. Jesus then reminds them that God is the God of the living, not of the dead, hoping that they will draw their own conclusions from this logic. He then smiles their way and tells them they are "badly mistaken." Ouch.

They are mistaken in two ways, their misappropriation of Scripture, and their underestimation of God as a life-giving, resurrecting power. Along with the Pharisees and Herodians they are trying to bring Jesus down. The fiery zeal of religious causes is known to burn hot and strong. Jesus will not be burned at the stake, but that is only because the religious "fundamentalists" and their friends have a better way of doing in Jesus that does not require as much wood.

MARK 12:28–37
MORE QUESTIONS: WHAT IS THE GREATEST COMMANDMENT AND WHO IS THE CHRIST?

Just when we are getting the impression that the desire to "get" Jesus is widespread among the religious leadership, Mark introduces us to a scribe, or a teacher of the law, who really listens and seems to want to understand Jesus. The question he asks Jesus starts out like many that come before it, and seems to be another trick question.

"Of all the commandments, which is the most important?" Is this like asking a parent at the family meal, "Which child do you love most?"

The end of this encounter, however, reveals a man who really is interested in Jesus' answer. Unlike the others we have read about who ask Jesus questions, this seeker wants to know Jesus' interpretation of Scripture.

This may be a good lesson for those of us who take religion seriously. When we engage in the area of interpretation of Scripture, do we come to it with an open mind or have we made up our minds before we start? Are we asking questions of the text, but under our breath we are saying, "Don't confuse me with the facts"?

This man who approaches Jesus is open to what Jesus has to say. Jesus links love of God with love of self and neighbor in his answer. This linkage is nothing new in Jesus' day. Other teachers have already done this.

What this answer does is allow Jesus to affirm his Jewish beliefs. He is not trying to be a rock thrower. Jesus loves his tradition. He remembers what he was taught in "Sunday school."

He begins his answer with the "pledge of allegiance" to the faith that every Jewish boy knows by heart. The "Shema" is the creed of the Jewish faith. Jesus recites his creed. He is a follower of the God of Abraham, Isaac, and Jacob. He is not a follower of religious leaders who cover over the true meaning and life of the faith with their own customs and legalistic details.

The words of Jesus in these few verses about putting love of God first, followed by neighbor and self, can be our homework for the rest of our lives. It is meant to be. Not only are the individual parts important, but the connection between, and balance of, love for God, neighbor, and self is critical.

To study the history of the Christian faith is to view the various ways that different generations have not balanced the relationship between these three loves. Unbalanced love of God can lead to narrow piety. Unbalanced love of neighbor can lead to social action without a tie to the transcendent reality from which it should spring. Unbalanced love of self leads to greed and an excessive thirst for power.

The imbalance can go in the opposite direction. Lack of love for God can lead to a disregard for the sacredness of life. Lack of love for neighbor can lead to a "what's in it for me" attitude that allows people to live on islands of self-satisfaction. Lack of real love of self can lead to a low self-esteem so that people are always trying to make up for something rather than learning to be the child of God they are created to be.

Jesus has it right, and this teacher of the law knows it. The scribe affirms Jesus' words and asserts that living out this commandment "to love God with all the heart, and with all the understanding, and with all the strength," and "to love one's neighbor as oneself" is more important than all the "burnt offerings and sacrifices." Such an assertion coming from one of the teachers of the law is quite a statement.

Remember these words are being said in the confines of the Temple: that place which stays in business because of burnt offerings and sacrifices. Those who make their living off such offerings and sacrifices hear one of their own starting to get the picture. This is not good. It is one thing for the rabble to say "Amen" to Jesus. It is quite another thing when someone who should know better starts saying "Amen."

In the next section, making things even worse, Jesus takes the offensive by pulling a Sadducee card from the deck. As he is teaching, Jesus quotes some Scripture to counter a point about the Messiah needing to be "son of David." The point Jesus makes is a technical one and does not sound like the Jesus that the rest of Mark presents.

What we have here is some version of the controversy that surrounds Mark's own community of faith about whether or not the Messiah needs to be a son of David. In Mark's Gospel there is no genealogy putting Jesus in the direct line of David. Some in Mark's community may not think it to be important.

The other issue we are dealing with here is the kind of expectation that many people have in Jesus' day of what the Messiah will be like. The version of the Messiah that most people are expecting is the kind of son of David who will set up David's rule whereby Israel would again be on top. David had been the most powerful King to have ruled over Israel. His effective military leadership and organizational skills had made of Israel a strong Empire for about a century. (Read more about David's story in 1 Sam. 16:13—1 Kings 2:12.)

Jesus does not meet these expectations. He points out to his listeners that David actually calls the Messiah "Lord," which means that the Messiah is greater than both David and the expectations that surround the kind of "son of David" leader that so many of the people want.

Jesus' death on a cross will crush most of the people's expectations about a Davidic Messiah. Jesus is preparing them for the house of cards to fall.

MARK 12:38-44
THE WIDOW'S OFFERING

I have attempted to show that throughout the Gospel of Mark there is a theme of Jesus' words constantly being misunderstood. Many Christians today become adept at this habit of misunderstanding. One of the most prominent examples of the misunderstanding of Jesus' words I have witnessed is the story of the "widow's mite." How many times have I heard, "I know what I give to the church may be the widow's mite, but that is the best I can do with what I have."

Go back and read the story. This is not a story about a woman who gives a small amount. This is a story about the kind of giving that is ridiculous and outrageous. This woman gives "everything she had, all she had to live on." If you want to find a biblical justification for giving a small amount to the church, please look somewhere else. This story will not help you.

Jesus, who is himself about to give all he has, points out that this woman gives from her poverty. He compares this gift to the large amounts that others have put in, but which don't make a dent in their finances or lifestyles. Jesus implies that those who have it to give but who give a small amount are, in fact, only tipping God.

Jesus notices the widow's devotion and sacrifice and calls his disciples over to make sure that they have noticed. Jesus wants his disciples to put a sign up at his church after he is gone which reads, "No Tipping Allowed." To make an example out of someone is usually thought of in negative terms. Jesus makes an example out of this dear woman, an example which the centuries cannot forget. Misunderstand, yes, but not forget.

A few verses later, Jesus is going to say that the very institution that this woman has given her all to will be destroyed. Maybe he should run up to her and say, "Ma'am, you would be better served by giving your money directly to some service agency rather than trusting this institution."

Those words are on the lips of some people today who do not trust the church. Jesus allows this woman to give her two coins because he knows that God sees into the heart of the giver. Churches hopefully spend the money given to them wisely, but even if they do not, the gift is still noticed by God. This is not to condone, however, the manipulative tactics of certain religious leaders who try to con older people out of their last dime, which then goes to line their own pockets.

In fact, another way of understanding this passage is to look at the story of the widow's mite in light of the few verses that come before it. In these verses, Jesus is criticizing the scribes who are walking around in fine clothes, wanting the best for themselves, and "devouring widows' houses."

Some Bible commentators think that Jesus draws attention to the widow who is giving her all as a way of condemning the religious system's demand for so much from those who are some of the poorest in society.

The widow walks out from the Temple in an even more precarious position while the scribes and other Temple leaders benefit personally from her donation. God's particular concern for widows can be seen throughout the Old Testament, the Gospels, and early church teachings.

Help me make this woman the saint that she is rather than allowing her to be used as the poster child for all those who are looking for a model of giving a small amount to the church. She is a model because of her deep devotion to God and to God's work. If more people give even close to the proportion that this woman gives, I would never have to preach another "money sermon." That would make a lot of people happy—even me.

Chapter Thirteen

MARK 13:1-37
THE SKY IS FALLING: THE END TIMES

Some people wonder if God made the human appendix simply to give surgeons something to take out. No one is sure why the appendix is there. It seems to serve no purpose except to make trouble when it becomes inflamed.

I sometimes feel that way about apocalyptic literature. Apocalyptic literature is what we are dealing with in chapter thirteen. It is as if Jesus is conversing in English and then all of a sudden he starts speaking in Russian. His language changes and his images become stark and mysterious.

Many people ignore these words about "the end." When they are highlighted, like our appendix they seem to cause trouble. Jesus' words are used by countless preachers to point to signs all around us that the end times are near at hand.

Like a biblical surgeon, I might desire to cut out these troublesome and troubling words for the health of the body of Christ. I cannot do that, but I am going to state that many people allow these words to cause much more concern that they merit.

Perhaps many of us can relate to the disciples who are continually misunderstanding Jesus' words, as we see throughout Mark. What does Jesus mean by these scary and strange sounding images of "the desolating sacrilege," false prophets, the moon not giving light and the stars falling from the sky?

We are entering a different time and place in chapter thirteen, much like the old TV program which announces, "You are now entering the Twilight Zone." When we hear the word "apocalyptic" we are to prepare ourselves for something different. The rules change. We must put on our 3D glasses in order to see. We need help in order to understand: an interpreter if you please.

In the absence of the glasses, or an interpreter, various people will tell you what all these images and "predictions" mean. Various seers do this immediately after Mark pens these words. Many are wrong about what they think Jesus means. All are wrong who use Jesus' words as a road map to when the world will end.

We know that the Temple, which is the trigger point for Jesus' remarks in chapter thirteen, is destroyed by the Romans in 70 AD at the time of the Jewish revolt. Jesus' words do come true, almost immediately. "The world" does come to an end for many people.

You can understand this if you ponder a moment what "the world" is to you. How many people's world comes to an end when a child dies, or a longtime business suddenly shuts down, or the words from the doctor's lips are "The test results are not good"?

For the followers of Jesus, then, the destruction of the Temple is a definite "end." It is not, however, "The End," the end of time. And this is the problem we have in this mysterious chapter.

Jesus warns that "The End" is coming soon, but not yet. The time is at hand but much must happen before it comes. For all those who want to make time lines and charts, he categorically states that "no one knows, neither the angels in heaven, nor the Son, but only the Father." Jesus is of course not privileged to live in the present day with all of our expertise and knowledge. It seems that some people today *do* know. All you have to do is go to the bookstore or turn on the TV and you can find people who have broken the code and have proven Jesus wrong. They have figured it out.

Listen carefully to the words of Jesus, "Beware that no one leads you astray." Many people are like poor little sheep who have lost their way when it comes to listening to those who have figured it out.

In this chapter, the words of Jesus describe events that have happened and that are happening in Mark's community of faith. Brother is against brother, people are being delivered up to both civil and religious councils, and wars and rumors of wars are everywhere. Many scholars think that at the time of Mark's writing, false messiahs are literally making claims about knowing the code for the end.

Jesus uses language that is familiar to him, although it is not so familiar to us. There is apocalyptic literature in the Bible that Jesus is aware of. The book of Daniel represents this genre. Most apocalyptic literature is written at times of national stress and focuses on the end of time. This style of language is on the buffet of techniques that Jesus has at his disposal. Jesus chooses to use apocalyptic language in a limited way.

He could make great use of it. The people are hungry for words that will tell them that the kind of tribulation they are living in is significant and is part of the end. The people are reaching for meaning in the midst of what often looks like a situation of "God is not in control, the world is."

Mark's portrayal of Jesus resists stepping into the contemporary expectations of what the Messiah will be. For many, the Messiah will be a magical, apocalyptic figure who will mysteriously and powerfully change things in an instant. God will swoop down and radically change the present order. The faithful will be lifted out of their suffering.

Jesus comes, and rather than swooping down, gets swept up on a cross. Mark's job is to show that, although it looks like he gets swept up, Jesus offers himself of his own will. Mark wants to show that the Christ suffers for the people and with the people. The hoped-for magic will not happen, but God is still in charge of the present and the future.

Some scholars think that Jesus' words in chapter thirteen were never spoken by him. They speculate that the words are not in keeping with the rest of the book. Some observers speculate that chapter thirteen is an insertion by Mark, after events have taken place, to help his own community put things into perspective. Although these speculations are interesting, I am not going to enter this debate. For the purposes of this book, I would rather we deal with the words in the text as we have them.

Despite Jesus' assurance in verse 30, the current generation does pass away before all these things take place. Does Mark think the end is on his own horizon? Perhaps he does. If so, this is a lesson for us to remember that the Bible is an ongoing revelation. It is a living word as well as a given word. God expects us to do what is inside the parentheses in verse 14, "Let the reader understand." Scripture is not supposed to always be easy to understand.

If these words, or ones similar to them, are spoken by Jesus, he expects his hearers to recognize the special apocalyptic language, and put on their 3D glasses in order to see. Apocalyptic language is different. It is not meant to be understood in a regular way. To do so misrepresents the intent of the highly symbolic nature of the language.

Jesus uses phrases from "the apocalyptic manual" to give people hope, "The days will be shortened for the sake of the faithful" (verse 20). This is classic apocalyptic language used to convey the reality that God will not forget the faithful even though the days of suffering seem long. God will bring an end to those days of suffering and tribulation.

We are in the midst of "birth pangs" (verse 8). That is where we live. When we die we are delivered. All of life is a kind of labor. Worlds do end. Challenges to our faith are constant. The temptation to be led astray is ever present.

Jesus' closing words are the ones we need to listen to in a day when so many are speaking about "The End." He simply says we must always watch and be ready, like today is our last. I heard someone say, "Live every day like it is your last, because someday you will be right."

God is at the beginning and at the end of every day. As smart as we are, we do not know much about significant "endings." That is in God's hands.

Jesus' words in chapter 13 must be treated with respect, and must be treated carefully. Our "generation will not pass away" until we see many signs if we will pay attention. The ultimate end always has been and still is in God's hands. We have other things to do than to be found trying to count days or predict events. Those who think they know more than Jesus have always been wrong—and always will be.

As a pastor I have been with people when life falls apart and "the stones of the Temple" crumble. I stand with families when "the moon does not shine" and "the stars fall" in their lives. I often feel the birth pangs of life and hold hands of those "in labor." Life with its various births and deaths can be painful, but it is still worth it. That's life. Life is in God's hands. The end of time, and all our endings are in God's hands. Watch. Wake up. Do not sleepwalk through life. There is much to do. Be ready every day. That is what Jesus says.

Chapter Fourteen

MARK 14:1-11
JESUS' ANOINTING

Mark is now ready to focus in on the last days of Jesus. It is time to draw open the curtain and position all the main characters on the stage.

Somewhat like the irony of calling for a ceasefire on Christmas day while knowing that fighting will begin again the day after, the religious leaders conspire to kill Jesus, but they do not want to do it during the feast days because it might upset the people. "Let's kill him—but let's wait until after the holidays."

The chief priests and scribes do not want to do anything that will spoil the significance of the high, holy days. Jesus will not go along with their plan. He steps into their waiting trap and sets it off right in the middle of Passover, the very time when the people are remembering and commemorating the story of their deliverance from slavery in Egypt. (Read more about this foundational story in Exodus 12:1–13:16.)

Mark makes sure the drama is played out on the same stage as the one where the Passover lambs are being sacrificed. Jesus is to die right alongside the Passover lambs. This is the "Aha!" of the Gospel. Mark wants his readers to see clearly that Jesus' death is connected symbolically to the Passover celebration, whose key themes are liberation from bondage and redemption.

On one side of the stage the spotlight illuminates a small scene of a woman who breaks open a jar of costly ointment and anoints Jesus' head. This woman spends what is the equivalent of a whole year's wages on this anointing, which Mark presents as a preliminary funeral for Jesus.

Nard is a spice of death. The woman pours the nard liberally over Jesus' head, provoking with her act of devotion a passionate debate about funeral expenses. Jesus quiets the debate by saying, "Cut the woman

116

some slack, folks. In the total scheme of things you will never miss this money, and besides, long after your words are forgotten, her gift of love and sacrifice will be remembered." He is right.

Yes, the ointment could have been sold and used for the poor, but Jesus knows something that one of his servants would later know. Mother Teresa, who worked so long and devotedly with the poor, once said that if she only had two pennies to spend for the poor, with one she would buy bread and with the other she would buy a flower. The poor need both bread and beauty.

Jesus is poor. He does not ask to be served. He allows this woman to step over the line this one time and he calls such extravagance beautiful.

We do not have the privilege of knowing just what is going on in the mind of Jesus as he steps toward the cross. Observing actions around him can give us a clue. In Mark's Gospel he usually declines the honor that comes his way, but now Jesus is preparing to give it all up. Even Jesus, the ultimate servant, now allows this woman to serve him. There will be no wake at his funeral. There will be no receiving line where friends file by and tears are exchanged. Casserole dishes will not be returned to those who have filled them with reminders of love.

Jesus will be alone in his death. This unnamed woman keeps him company. Is she the only one who gets it? All the men around Jesus seem to either be in denial or just plain dense. It is a woman's heart and a woman's eyes that see and feel the depth of what is unfolding. Jesus allows such love to be given. Even a suffering servant is allowed a gift of love.

The other scene that takes place on stage for this final act unfolds at the back, almost behind the curtain. The spotlight shines on this scene but all that is witnessed are shadowy figures with their backs to the audience. Judas and the chief priests know that they need to be near the back of this scene until the time is right to throw open the curtain and take charge of the final act. They want the timing of this drama to coincide with a final scene that will conclude this messy episode. They will discover that when the curtain falls it has a tear in it, a tear they never noticed before.

MARK 14:12-25
THE LAST SUPPER

While serving my first pastorate, I opened the door of my office one morning and discovered that someone had broken in the night before. After examining the area, I surmised that the only thing missing was a portable communion set. This set was a small black box which opened to reveal three small communion glasses, a tiny plate for wafers, and a small bottle for the juice. In the lid of the box was an engraving of the Last Supper.

Evidently the thief thought the box was some kind of electronic device, probably a tape player. In his haste, and with the lights out, he probably thought it was worth the taking since no money would be discovered missing, and besides, my religious books were not a very tempting commodity.

I would love to have seen the thief's face when he opened the black box only to find Jesus looking back at him. What a disappointment and a surprise.

So we have this scene of Jesus and his disciples gathered around the table in the large upstairs guest room, preparing to eat the Passover meal. He is looking out at us with disappointment on his face. The world he looks into, both then and now, is one of betrayal and denial.

Jesus looks into the faces of the small band of men he has chosen to carry on his work. He sees those who have argued over who would be the greatest in the kingdom. He observes Peter, the fiery leader who will soon deny that he even knows Jesus. Reclining somewhere around the table is Thomas who, according to John's Gospel, will doubt to the end and even beyond. The whole bunch of them will later in this dark night, run and hide in order to save their hides.

Judas is the focus of this cosmic irony. Mark has Judas play his part. Jesus says that this is the way the script is written. It is almost as if Judas tried out for the role and got it. Why blame the actor? In the rock opera *Jesus Christ Superstar*, Judas complains to Jesus that the betrayal is part of a plan that he is swept up in. He pleads not to be damned for all time. The audience is pulled into a sympathetic response for Judas.

We will never know Judas' motives. Mark seems not to care. In this final scene, Judas is a bit player. Mark does not even bother to tell us what happens to Judas. When the lights fade after the fatal kiss, Judas simply disappears from the stage leaving us with pen in hand to write stories about why he has done it.

The reversals around this table, where Jesus and his disciples are reclining, sharing their last meal together, are almost more than can be taken in. Jesus takes life-giving bread and speaks to them of death. He lifts a full cup and paints a scene of emptiness. He offers the first dip in the cup to the very person who will betray him. He tells his disciples that he will drink no more until he enters that new kingdom where his cup will overflow.

It is no wonder the disciples do not take in all this. Can anyone? Have we made this last supper so routine that we miss its costly drama? This man, who contains all of God that any human can contain, is eating with his best friends, and talking to them about the end, and they do not get it. He is showing them that "power" and "glory" are not as they would have it. Instead he shares with them the blessed, broken bread, and the poured-out wine.

Jesus brings to the world a different understanding of power and glory. The kind of power and glory that Judas and his other followers, and maybe even we as a church, want for Jesus is not the kind that he sees for himself.

Later in the rock opera, in the second part of the song *Simon Zealotes/Poor Jerusalem,* Jesus' haunting response to Simon's plea that he assume the power and glory he is due is that there is absolutely no one who understands what power and glory are. His punch line is, "It is only by dying that death is overcome."

The thief who broke into my office is not the first person to experience disappointment when facing Jesus. Life often throws an unexpected curve. The crux of the gospel, however, happens in the midst of this dramatic disappointment. Life will come from death. Hope will come from despair. Wholeness will come from brokenness. Courage will break forth from denial and betrayal.

What is important for Mark is that the disappointment is the source of our salvation. This is the motif of his entire Gospel. Mark is writing in the midst of all the questions which have arisen from the disappointment that Jesus is not the kind of Messiah that the people are hoping for. Denial, betrayal, and crucifixion by the Romans are not elements in the script that the people are reading and writing.

In this meal, Jesus represents the reality that God does not stop bad endings or do away with suffering. Jesus lifts the cup for every one of our deep disappointments. That is why—if my thief friend had stopped long enough to look at his surprise find that night in my office—he would have caught a glimpse of the gospel message in all its irony and power. Jesus would have looked into his eyes and said, "I am doing this for you."

That is what Jesus says to those first disciples, Judas included. This act of love is God's meal placed on the table for all God's children. It becomes *the* meal for Christians. Jesus' last supper becomes, in a sense, the "first supper."

In Mark's community, the commemoration of this last supper is already happening. Many of Mark's readers, as they hear how the story has its beginning, are already feasting at his table. They are wondering how long it will be before the new kingdom will come. They have no way of knowing that we who read the story today are still anticipating that coming.

Many in the Christian community seem to focus on the idea that "Jesus is coming soon." Mark's own community is probably caught up in this expectation. The other Gospels, which are written later, spend time and words trying to interpret the delay of this anticipated second coming.

There is so much kingdom work to be done today that it is again time to give "the Day of the Lord" to the one to whom it belongs. Some kind of cosmic wrap-up is not our concern. We always live "in between times." We live in between the time we were crafted by God and the time we will return to God. That's all there is to it.

We can watch and wait for the second coming, but the time for participating in the kingdom is now. While we pray for God's will to be done "on earth as it is in heaven," we also have a responsibility to use our gifts and abilities to work towards bringing about God's vision of heaven on Earth.

Today is the time to struggle with the reversals that Jesus inaugurates at this last meal. We are servants of a gospel that speaks of the least among us being the most important, about finding the power and glory in brokenness, in being poured out. We are called to sit at the table with all kinds of people, betrayers, liars, cowards, foreigners—fill in the blank. Many Christians will not sit down at the table with some who Jesus still calls his friends. These include gay people, people living with

AIDS, people of different color or economic status, immigrants—yes legal and illegal—and the list goes on...or does it, for you?

We need to focus again on the Lord's Table and realize that he still calls around him all those who will eat, drink, and remember. Open the lid of that box which contains the Last Supper, look into his eyes, and you will know that we each share something in common with my thief friend. We grab life as if it is ours to take. However, life is a gift that must be received gratefully, shared, and then given back.

That is some of what this meal was and is about. Jesus speaks the words in these verses that make it so, "Take, eat . . . drink . . . this is given for you."

MARK 14:27–42
JESUS TELLS PETER OF HIS DENIAL/THE GARDEN SCENE

Poor old Peter, he reminds me of a small child who wants to please. He so wants to be the leader of Jesus' small tribe. He is almost always the first to speak. He wants to be brave, but he does not understand that he must face his fear in order to obtain courage.

Like the lion in the *Wizard of Oz*, he paws at imaginary enemies as if to fight them, but he does not recognize his own demons of self-doubt. Jesus looks straight into Peter's eyes and pulls the demon of fear from within Peter's soul. Jesus then dangles this kicking and screaming internal monster in front of Peter.

Peter shadow boxes the fear and boldly tells Jesus that the title fight is over and the victory is obtained. In the face of Jesus' prediction that all the disciples would become deserters, Peter makes an assertion that leaves himself open for a left jab. Peter announces, "Maybe the rest of these losers will desert you, but I am your main man, and I will never leave you."

Jesus tells Peter that before the last bell rings Peter will not even come out of his corner to fight. The spotlight will fall on his empty stool in the corner of the ring and Peter will be gone.

Peter refuses to listen to the truth of Jesus' words. This scene reminds me of a line in the movie, *A Few Good Men*. A young lawyer is questioning a Marine Colonel, played by Jack Nicholson, about the rigid and cruel training practices that those under his command have had to follow. The young lawyer has Nicholson on the ropes, and this

Marine leader, who believes in training the fear out of recruits by using fear itself, becomes angry.

"What is it you want?" Nicholson says to the young lawyer.

"I want the truth," the lawyer responds.

"You can't handle the truth!" screams Nicholson.

The enraged Marine commander then goes on to explain that in order to prepare people to kill the enemy, the trainers use techniques that are not so civilized and pretty. Those who sit back home enjoying freedom do not want to know what it takes to protect that freedom. They "can't handle the truth."

Peter cannot handle the truth. This night the truth for Peter is not a pretty sight.

Next we have the scene where drama melts in the light of reality. My imagination drifts toward the question, "How did the writer come to know what happens in that garden?" The only eyewitness to this event is the one Jesus calls, "Abba."

Does Jesus sit Peter down after the resurrection and tell him what transpired after they all went to sleep? Perhaps Jesus' narration of how he pleaded for his life comes just after that scene in John's Gospel when Jesus, after his resurrection, fixes breakfast for the disciples.

In John's Gospel there is a dramatic encounter between Jesus and Peter with the three "Do you love me?" questions. Could it be that Jesus, seeing how deeply disappointed Peter is to be reminded three times of his all-too-human inability to love, leans over to this leader of the new mission and whispers to him what happened that night in the garden just before they all ran?

Maybe Jesus wants Peter to know of the passion and the longing that come out when Jesus is alone with himself and his Abba. Jesus too wants to live. He is afraid. Could it be that this Messiah wants the one who is to hold the "keys to the kingdom" to know that even a Messiah can be afraid?

Peter, the one who denies knowing Jesus, is to be the one who will need to stay awake while the world thinks it can sleep. In Peter's future, many people will want to rub the sleep from their eyes and call the whole episode a bad dream. Peter will be the leader who will need to proclaim that it is no dream.

Someone gains access to the details of this scene in the garden. Jesus bargains with God. He wrestles with an angel like his ancestor Jacob, and like Jacob, he too limps away from his ordeal. Finding his disciples asleep, Jesus returns to his solitary place of prayer. He boldly asks again for the cup to pass. No harm in asking. After all, Jesus tells his disciples to be bold in asking God for things.

How many times have I told people that they may as well ask God for what they want? It is on their hearts anyway. It is not like we can hide our thoughts and longings behind some screen. "Be honest with your prayers," I say, "but remember what happens in the garden. Jesus ends his plea with "not my way but your way."

This is God we are dealing with, not some judge in a "Who Can Pray Better?" contest. To say, "not my will but thine be done" is an admission that God is God and we are not. Jesus helps us to see this by doing it this night in the garden—alone with God.

Jesus puts God on the spot in this prayer. Do you suppose there are words in response from God in the breeze this evening? Does Abba say, "My son, you can walk away from this. Go wake up your sleeping little band and leave before the guards come. It is up to you."

Jesus knows he can walk away. He is talking not only to his Abba, he is talking to himself. He is wrestling with the same dilemma that you and I often battle. To walk the road less traveled does make all the difference. God will not make us take that road, but taking it can lead to needed results.

Jesus pleads not only for himself, he pleads for us. Because Jesus desires another way, we are allowed to desire another way. It is not wrong to do so. His pleas are for us in our solitude, for those times when we may wish that those around would be sleeping so as not to hear our hopes and pleas for self-preservation.

We keep this in balance with other words from this same Messiah when he says, "To find your life you may need to lose it." On this night, however, his agony is for us when we know the right way is the hard way, but we hunger to go the easy way.

I have this picture of Jesus standing over the sleeping disciples. He looks down at bundles of bodies who are tired of it all. Mark has an interesting way of painting this picture with his words. He writes, "And once more he came and found them sleeping, for their eyes were very heavy; and they did not know what to say to him." (Verse 40)

These sleeping disciples have no more words of reply to predicted denials and betrayals. This time the denial is the kind that comes with grief. They long to escape the heaviness of an evening that is hemmed in with words about "body and blood." Their sleep and silence speaks loudly to a pondering Messiah as he looks down at his tired bunch. Their silence screams, "We do not want to hear anymore. We have nothing left to say . . . and yes, we can't handle the truth."

But Jesus breaks open their grief and denial with more words. He speaks the very word they long to hear, but his meaning is different than the hope for which they long. "Enough," he says. Oh, how they long for it to be enough, but Jesus awakens them to yet another beginning of the end. "It's time to get on with it," he says into their sleep-filled eyes.

Jesus has told them about the previews of coming attractions. It is now time for the feature presentation. They awake to one of their own coming toward them leading a mob. It is no bad dream. No longer can they watch. They are now part of the feature presentation whether they want to be or not.

MARK 14:43–52
THE ARREST

His name was Jimmy. He was one of my childhood playmates. When he was afraid he got mad. He would turn his face away from me and swing wildly. It was a sad sight, a young boy trying to show courage but not being able to look into the eyes of his adversary.

One of the disciples plays this part the night of Jesus' arrest. The disciple swings wildly and wounds one of the mob. The blow is symptomatic of the entire event. It is an errant swing into the night with no intention of really changing anything. With one swing of a sword the curtain falls on a group of disciples who feel they are powerless.

With this poor slave's ear still bleeding, the disciples run into the night. They strike a blow for liberty only to find that they are captive to their fears and their crushed hopes.

Judas kisses Jesus, which has all the pathos of shining headlights into the eyes of a deer in the dark of night and then pulling the trigger while the animal is still blinded. Judas never gets over this kiss.

Mark leaves it to other Gospel writers to tell of Judas' death. In Mark's story we never hear about Judas again. He blends in to the crowd and is lost.

My imagination tells me that Judas ends up wishing he did not kiss Jesus. Such a move brought their eyes together. Judas' last memory is of those eyes looking into his. There is another wounding this night which is not portrayed by Mark. Judas' heart leaps as he looks into Jesus' eyes.

Judas should simply point him out. The kiss does him in. He gets too close to Jesus. As Judas puts his hands on Jesus' shoulders, he feels the warm sweat on the body of Jesus. The man Judas now holds in his grasp was, a few moments earlier, pleading for his own life. Judas feels that life pouring from Jesus' body. That life feels warm and liquid.

When Judas draws back from Jesus after the kiss, all is different. Nothing will ever be the same. As the mob takes Jesus away, all that Judas hears is an echo of those strange words, "This is my body and blood."

Jesus looks into the faces of the mob and reminds them that he has been available for the taking on many occasions in the Temple. Why are they now treating him as a criminal? "Let the scriptures be fulfilled," he says into the night. And Judas wonders what his part is in those scriptures.

Mark closes this scene with the description of a "certain young man" who ends up running away from the grasp of one of the guards, leaving behind his only garment. This mysterious character of the night is similar to the Mona Lisa's coy smile. No one knows who or why.

Mark wants us to speculate about this naked character but leaves us only with the questions. Like the guard in this scene, we are left holding the cloth. We can clothe this shadowy figure in all sorts of garments, but ultimately we are left with Mark's own mysterious smile.

Yes, the naked runner could be you or me. Is Mark here asking a question of the reader? Is this figure placed here to remind us of our own ability to watch from a distance and then run when someone pulls us too close to the steps that lead to a cross? I shall resist the sermon that could be preached. I will leave you with Mark's own smile. That is as it should be. Mark's Gospel gives many answers, but it also asks many questions.

MARK 14:53-72
THE TRIAL AND THE DENIAL

There is a method of discernment called "trial and error." What we have in the trial of Jesus is trial *by* error. The trial of Jesus is similar to the trial given to many African Americans at the hands of the KKK earlier in this century. The only evidence needed in such late evening "trials" conducted by costumed Klansman is the evidence provided by one's skin color. The reality of a cross burning in the background and the "criminal" being present provides a foregone conclusion.

Jesus' trial is simply a means to an end. Jesus is asked a couple of questions, a few "witnesses" are called, and a kind of jury is there to listen. This is only done to give the morning papers something to print so that the lynching will be veiled behind the semblance of a trial.

Mark finally allows Jesus to say he *is* the Messiah. No sooner than the words are out of his mouth, Jesus adds these words of transcendence, "'You will see the Son of Man seated at the right hand of the Power,' 'coming with the clouds of heaven.'"

Mark's first hearers are ready for this to happen. They want the heavens to open up and the whole thing to be wrapped up with a happy ending. Mark's own listeners are enduring their own trials. They are being tempted, as Peter is tempted, to say that they do not know this Jesus.

What Mark's hearers do not realize is that the first part of Jesus' prediction is coming true in the present tense. His power is being made manifest by the loyalty of Mark's audience. The authorities that "do in" Jesus will try to regain the power, but what Jesus starts will not die.

The "coming with the clouds" part—well—that becomes the stuff of gospel songs. Many are still wondering what the coming with the clouds stuff means. Christians for centuries have looked at the clouds and have seen all kinds of shapes in those clouds. Imaginative schemes have been devised.

I think Jesus still wants us to look at the clouds in order to remember the transcendent, "outside and beyond," nature of God's plan. While we are part of that plan, God is the one behind it all. Beyond the clouds is mystery. We simply do not know. The future is God's. We may think we see shapes in those clouds but it is what is beyond the clouds that matters.

We, who do not shape the clouds, must embrace the first part of Jesus' promise, that we "will see him seated at the right hand of the Power." That power is available to us, especially in times of trial and temptation. One day, each of us will participate in the "beyond" part of reality. We shall meet him "in the clouds." To make this image literal is to create our own shapes in the clouds. Let us leave that to God.

Jesus is condemned after some dramatic posturing by the High Priest who really gets into his part and tears his clothes. He gets the award for overacting. Such a gesture is not really needed but perhaps it makes for a great photo op.

The High Priest then shouts to the crowd the most understated question ever, about whether or not Jesus is deserving of death, "What is your decision?" That question is about as superfluous as asking, "Is the Pope Catholic?"

Things get really nasty very quickly. The flood waters are building up and this is the first opportunity to open the gates of the dam. Jesus is awash with hate. They began to spit on him. They blindfold him, ridicule him, and start taking swings at him.

This crowd is ready. This is no spontaneous inciting of a mob. They are poised to strike. They are like runners who are in the kneeling position at the starting line waiting for the pistol shot. Their muscles are quivering, for the race has been constantly delayed. When the High Priest tears his clothes, the race begins. At its end is a cross, and the crowd is just dying to get there. The whole race is about dying.

Meanwhile, in Mark's customary literary style, there is another storyline ready to be played out. Peter is in the courtyard outside. He is warming his hands beside a fire. His heart is beating wildly, but his heart is cold. Things are happening too fast. Peter is a quick talker but at this moment his thoughts are muddled and confused. He is often quick to speak, but that is when he is in control. He senses that he is not now in control of what is happening.

His tunic is wrapped around his face for he wants no one to recognize him. He is there only as a spectator. He wants to know what is going to happen so that he can plan his next move, but a servant-girl makes the first move.

"You were with this Jesus from Nazareth!" Peter hears that name. His cold heart is suddenly thrown into the middle of that fire. As if she tossed some of the burning embers into his face, he jerks away. "I do not know or understand what you are talking about," he says.

Ah Peter, you speak the truth in a strange way. At least you finally admit that you do not understand or know what is happening. No longer are you sure of what should happen. In fact, Peter, you are now feeling that you are not sure of anything, especially yourself.

What you need now is to be left alone. This is not the time for another question, but this curious woman will not let you be. Like a horse fly honing in on its prey, she follows you away from the fire.

This time the pesky woman speaks to the crowd. "He can't fool me. I'll take bets that he is one of them." Peter, you think the woman a pest, what about that rooster crowing in the background? Now things are rushing toward you like stampeding animals.

Your answers are becoming shorter. "No," is all you can muster. The crowd seems to want to close in on you. You need some space. The air is getting thin. Your breath is short.

And then you explode. It is as if the bystanders jump you and you have to fight them back. You begin to scream. Your statements take on color. In response to the next accusation, you swear an oath. If this scene was being played out in a modern day barroom and you had been cornered with a nasty lie, you would have silenced everyone in the bar with a good, "God damn it! I don't know this guy!" (Don't get upset, it says "swear," and after all, this is God we are dealing with, remember.)

And then the mirror you are carrying around falls to the floor and shatters into pieces. Its crashing fades into the morning crow of that damned rooster. And after the crashing there is the silence, that awful silence.

You convince the bystanders. Their questions stop as if their only task is to have you lose your balance and drop the mirror. You look on the ground and peer into broken pieces of the mirror and you see your fractured self. Into your shaking hands you bury your twisted face.

But you weep not alone, Peter. We know. For there is a piece of your broken mirror into which we peer and we see not your image but ours. Go ahead and cry, Peter. We will cry with you. No one here condemns you. We know your denial all too well.

Chapter Fifteen

MARK 15:1–20
JESUS BEFORE PILATE/THE ABUSE BY THE SOLDIERS

Reading Mark at this point, one wants to slow things down. Events are transpiring too fast. But if you are pulling for Jesus, perhaps it is best that things are going so fast. Like standing beside the bed of a cancer patient who is in the last phase of the dreaded disease, one may wish the end to come quickly.

Jesus' condition is terminal. He is afflicted with incurable love. His obedience to the path of the suffering servant is a self-fulfilling prophecy. His love for his mission is going to be the death of him yet. Why not get it over with?

Those who possess the cure that could save Jesus have flushed it down the drain of the Temple. Pilate offers these very same men the chance to see if there is perhaps one vial of the saving antidote left. They all look at each other and say, "He's not worth the effort."

The official Jewish court brings Jesus to Pilate, who was the Roman procurator of the area from 26–36 AD. Mark wants everyone in on this act. Surely they can find a way to do him in. Jesus can accidentally fall down the steps just after his appearance before the Sanhedrin and break his neck. But Mark knows that crucifixion is a Roman punishment for disobedient slaves and political troublemakers. This is to be no accident.

In Mark's own community that is being persecuted by some of the Jewish leaders, it would be convenient to put the blame on the Jews, but that is not the way things actually happen. Jesus dies at the hands of the Romans even if the cheerleaders are Jewish. As an aside, I want to point out the importance of our not assigning blame to the Jewish people for what happens to Jesus. We must beware of any anti-Semitism which can lead to tragic consequences, as history has demonstrated.

The way that Mark paints the picture, Pilate would just as soon let Jesus go back to preaching. Those who condemn Jesus for religious crimes want Rome to do the dirty work for them. What a wonderful exit strategy. The Temple leaders get rid of this pesky, trouble-making prophet and blame it on "those horrible Romans." Everybody wins but Jesus and that is the idea.

All kinds of speculation can go into what kind of guy Pilate really is. Mark presents him as fairly benign, although history generally presents such procurators as ruthless. Judea is probably not the best assignment when it comes to governmental assignments.

Pilate has reasons to hate the whole lot of them. Maybe he is having a good day when they bring Jesus to him. Pilate says something like, "Listen up, Jesus. Are you this King of the Jews like they say you are? If you are, it's curtains. We have too many kings around here, and the truth is the only king that matters is my boss."

Jesus' answer seems bland compared to the gravity of the situation. Jesus replies, "It seems that's what everybody thinks." Pilate could say, "Wait a minute. Is that a yes or a no?"

Before Jesus gets a chance to say anything else, the peanut gallery erupts with chants accusing Jesus of being everything from a child molester to a member of the Jerusalem mafia. Pilate does not have any love lost for this peanut gallery so he turns back to Jesus and says, "You had better speak up, fella. You do not seem to have many friends in the room."

Then we have some of the saddest words in all the New Testament, "But Jesus made no reply." It is the silence of salvation. I do not particularly like it. How about at least some good counterpunches before the knockout blow is delivered?

Jesus just stands and takes the pounding. What kind of weakness is this? It is the weakness that will be God's way of offering a new way of life. I still do not like it, but then Jesus knows that. He knows we will not like it, but remember most of us are still back there with the guy who cut off the slave's ear. We want to get even.

Jesus keeps his mouth shut even though we have trouble doing the same. He stands there looking at Pilate and then looking at the angry peanut gallery. Jesus probably takes some deep breaths and says in a voice only he can hear, "It's happening, much like I thought it would."

And then perhaps he closes his eyes and prays so as to block out the sounds of what will happen next. Perhaps he does a guided meditation and allows his aching head to travel back to a day beside the Sea of Galilee when he was a boy. He skips some rocks across the water and watches a bird sail down toward a fishing boat. He wishes he were that bird.

Suddenly the bird's flight is halted by the sound of one word, "Crucify!" He hears the word over and over again. Somehow another name is introduced, a name he does not know, Barabbas.

Pilate tries one last time to fix things. "Look, I'm feeling generous today. How about if I honor your religious holiday by releasing one prisoner? This guy seems fairly harmless to me." But the crowd wants Barabbas, one of their own. The crowd decides that Jesus is not "one of their own."

But the crowd—ah yes, it is the crowd again—they want blood. The crowd is like the "they" in church. We are not sure who "they" are but "they" sure want Jesus crucified.

"Now about this Jesus, let's just call it a day," Pilate offers.

"No!" screams the crowd reading the cue cards from the chief priests, "We want him crucified. We came for a crucifixion and we do not want to go home empty-handed."

Pilate scratches his head—there is no washing of hands in Mark's Gospel—and pushes Jesus out toward the mob. Pilate is not in the mood to call out more soldiers who are on leave so he satisfies the crowd. He shakes his head in disbelief and says something like, "I don't understand you people. This guy seems guilty only of not wanting to defend himself, but, go on, have at him. What is one more crucifixion among many?"

Pilate then peers into the crowd's eyes and into the faces in the peanut gallery. He has condemned others to the cross and he does not want any more trouble or he will have to order a truck load of crosses and start stringing up some of the crowd. It has happened before, it could happen again.

Pilate walks off mumbling to himself, "Screwy people, they don't deserve a king. Let them see the one they *think* is king die for his foolish silence."

The soldiers, who have to work the holiday weekend, are not happy about having to work harder. Jesus becomes their outlet. If they had some automatic weapons, they would probably open up on the whole crowd. Most of these Roman soldiers are away from their families in this "godforsaken" land of the Jews . . . To heck with all of them.

Jesus becomes representative to them before he becomes representative for us. They start whipping up on him. "King, huh? Well let's get you some clothes, mister king." They grab a piece of cloth and one of the guards cuts off a rough twist of thorn bush and weaves a crown for this loser.

Another of the guards, who just finished reading a letter from his sweetheart informing him that she has found another love, grabs a stick and pushes it into Jesus' hands, and kneels before him shouting something like, "How about sending me back home, mister king?" The guard then stands up and spits into the face of Jesus and calls him a jerk.

It is not a pretty sight. Soldiers are capable of doing terrible things under the stress of being soldiers, especially to those who are the cause of their work.

After the soldiers vent, they look at the sundial and realize the time is getting late. One of them says, "Hell, let's get on with it—Grab those other two guys and let's do them all together. These folks want a crucifixion? Well let's give them three for the price of one."

No, it does not say this, but it might as well. What do you call mocking? This is called the "passion narrative" in the Gospel accounts. Use your imaginations to fill in the blanks. It is supposed to be passionate. Do not pretty it up. This scene is supposed to get our attention. It is the drama of salvation. Let it be dramatic.

MARK 15:21–41
THE CRUCIFIXION

I recently read an article written by a physician about the medical particularities of Roman crucifixion. The words are not for those who have a weak stomach. Death by crucifixion is meant to be slow and painful. It is more torture than execution.

The victim's feet are pushed upward and a ledge is provided behind the body to allow the criminal to push himself up to relieve pain. You may be thinking this is a touch of mercy, but the reality behind such a device is to prolong the pain since death usually comes by suffocation. Pushing up allows one to breathe longer and suffer more. Nice touch, huh?

Most of us have seen crucifixes a little too much. Crucifixes are frozen. I suggest you read these verses in Mark slowly and allow the words to melt the frozen image.

Mark does not go into detail. He seems to assume that the people who will read this account understand crucifixion. Later Gospel writers will elaborate this scene based on their traditions. Mark's picture is in pen and ink. He leaves the watercolors to other writers.

The picture is almost too simple. There are no "seven last words" here. As with the entire Gospel, Jesus speaks few words. He simply does the work of salvation. Various scriptures are fulfilled, especially from the Psalms. It is almost as if Mark wants us to watch in silence and not ask too many questions about details.

Everybody present, except for the women who have followed Jesus all along, mocks Jesus. Jesus may remain silent but the crowd still wants answers.

"Aren't you the guy who was going to destroy the Temple and build it back in three days? With tricks like that, it should not be difficult for you to do a disappearing act despite those nails that are keeping you up there."

"What's all this about 'saving' people? Sounds like a real good time to save yourself, mister King of Israel. So this is the 'Messiah' we have been waiting for, is it?"

Jesus makes no reply. He just hangs there between two "robbers," who according to Mark, join in the mockery. There is no repentant thief in Mark.

The picture is really bleak. Jesus is alone. Even dramatic trappings are torn away along with the veil of the Temple. Mark's Jesus dies without fanfare and is cradled in darkness. A cold front comes through and dark clouds hover overhead. Thunder creates the background. A lightning bolt strikes the very center of the Temple mount and the curtain in the Holy of Holies gets singed. The Temple's few remaining priests, who are not watching the main event down at Golgotha, wonder what all of this means.

Jesus is offered a mixture of wine and myrrh but he refuses it. He wants this over.

Simon of Cyrene watches from the bottom of this skull hill and whispers a prayer of thanksgiving that it is not him up there. Simon peers down at his own blood-stained tunic and wonders if the blood on the woven fabric is his or this stranger's whose cross he was just forced to carry.

It only takes six hours for Jesus to die. Six hours are not much in the scope of all eternity. If our theology is at all correct these are the longest six hours that God ever spends. Jesus is an only child. Only children have a way of being the center of attention to a parent. Can anyone imagine what God now feels? Perhaps God has second thoughts.

Does God bury his tired head in his hands and try to blank out the echoes of, "Abba, please . . . ?" All that God seems to come up with is some hellish thunder and lightning.

This is God's absence at its finest. It is that absence that calls forth Jesus' only words. Mystics and the rest of us deal in one way or another with this absence of God. Religious types try to clean up this silence or cover it up, but it is real—ask Jesus.

"My God, my God why have you forsaken me?" Yes, it is a quote from the Psalms. Jesus knows his Bible, but can he not pick some other verses that are much more inspiring to leave us with on such an occasion?

What Jesus speaks, however, is truth. He speaks to God for all of us in our times of forsakenness: when children die; when the medical test comes back bad; when the airplane crashes; when the tornado destroys the church; when a spouse says, "I don't love you anymore"; when pictures of Nazi death camps fill TV screens; when . . . well why don't you fill in the space here . . . this absent space . . . fill it in with your time of forsakenness.

But for now, back to his forsakenness. It is ironic that the people hearing Jesus misunderstand his dying words. They think he is calling for Elijah. This is great for the religious leaders who are responsible for hanging Jesus out to dry. Elijah, sure enough, is supposed to appear before the Messiah comes on the scene.

When the religious leaders hear Jesus calling Elijah, they ask that the volume be turned up so that all the people can hear this one last failure. They want to be able to make sure that at the morning press conference they can put an end to this trouble in the land. Elijah will not come and they know it.

The truth is that they no longer believe that Elijah will come for anybody. They have become encrusted with the cult of religion. These religious leaders are too far removed from hope. Hope is replaced with religion. All they know to give people are the rules and regulations that they have learned to lean on since the hope has been gone.

Calling on Elijah represents the old ways that are for the most part museum pieces of a way that is dead. "Let him utter the hope of the old ways for all the people to hear. Tomorrow we will get them back to reality."

But they misunderstand again. Jesus is not calling on the old ways. He is utterly in the present. He screams into the dark clouds which seem to be surrounding him. He screams for us. He is not calling on Elijah. He is calling on his "Abba."

Do not misunderstand him again. He screams for us. The absence is real, but God hears. Do you hear that? The absence is real, but God hears.

Jesus tells us in his dying breath that moments of abandonment will happen. Life's storms rain down on the just and the unjust. Jesus dies in the midst of the thunderous truth that life is full of glory and times of forsakenness—but God hears.

Maybe that is what the centurion senses as he watches this scene up close and personal. This nameless soldier who helps execute this "king" suddenly speaks strange words for a man with blood on his hands,

"Truly this man was the son of God."

Maybe this isolated soldier gains a rare respect for a dying man who can be honest with "the gods." Here at last is someone who can, with his dying breath, risk honesty with the power into whose hands he might be passing.

"Maybe you know something I don't know," thinks this soldier. "Could it be that what they say of you is true? Perhaps your relationship to whomever or whatever 'god' is, is deeper than anyone here imagines?"

The soldier is the only person on this black Friday who glimpses the truth. Jesus throws himself into the arms of his Abba. He knows he can be honest with his pain and his sorrow. He knows, as he feels this terrible absence, how much his Abba loves him. What Jesus knows even more is how much this Abba loves the people for whom his only son is dying.

This is the good news. This is gospel truth—and this is the simple, though painful, truth of this black and white picture that Mark paints.

MARK 15:42–47
THE BURIAL

Dead. It is a short word, a final word. It is a word that now describes Jesus. It is a word that surrounds his disciples and their hopes and dreams. It is a word that is whispered across the lips of the few faithful women who witness his death. It is a word that is mixed with the salty tears that gather around those women's lips as they speak silent prayers. He is dead.

Long before *Time* magazine printed the bold words "God Is Dead" across the cover years ago, these words surround a scene outside the walls of busy Jerusalem, on one of the many Passover festivals that this fought-over city has witnessed. Most people pay no attention to this lonely would-be prophet who dies quickly on a cross. For most of the religious pilgrims, Jesus is but a flash in the pan. He is one that could have fit the bill but he did not.

But for the few who risk believing that he might be the one, for those few, God is dead. Those few have poured their "God hopes" into this man. They believed he might be the one to redeem Israel. It is too early yet for complicated formulas which attempt to convey just how much of Jesus is God, but for these few people he is their last hope. At least part of God, the biggest part, the closest part, dies on a cross.

Soon, some of those who will be willing to risk believing that he is *the one* will question this death. Early on in the Christian tradition a belief in Docetism takes hold. Supporters of this claim have much to believe in when it comes to Jesus, but they cannot accept his death. They come up with all kinds of ways that Jesus avoids death. Some believe that Jesus' physical body and his crucifixion are illusions, others that someone else is crucified instead of Jesus, that at the last minute God pulls the real Jesus away from the weak and broken body that hangs on the cross. "Dead" is not the right word for God's only son.

For those who claim Docetism, resurrection is not necessary because Jesus never dies. He simply ascends back to his father from whom he came. It is a happy ending without the messy cross, but it is wrong. The early church stamps such belief as heresy. Mark's Gospel is written to help give evidence for the fact that Jesus, the son of God, dies.

Even Pilate has a hard time believing the fact. When Joseph of Arimathea goes to Pilate and courageously asks for the body of Jesus,

Pilate asks one of his death squad whether the poor soul is already dead. The guard assures Pilate that he is in fact quite dead.

In two verses Mark uses the word dead three times. Jesus is dead. For the moment, Jesus' followers and his teachings might as well be dead. A few weeping women stand by helplessly. The disciples are nowhere to be found. Passover is back to business as usual.

The solitary figure who reminds us that the kingdom of God is still the subject of the day is none other than one of the enemy. Joseph of Arimathea may be one about whom Marks says, "he is waiting expectantly for the kingdom of God," but he is also a respected member of the very group that signed the death warrant for Jesus.

Who knows Joseph's motives for not only showing up but putting up his own burial site for Jesus? Does Joseph believe that Jesus really is the one? In the midst of all the false witnesses, denials, and betrayals, does Joseph find himself looking out the window and saying to himself in between all the screaming, "My God, this really is the Messiah, and we are going to kill him?"

Is Joseph as helpless as the women who watch? Does he try to offer a counterargument in support of Jesus only to be crushed underneath the rolling boulder of fear and hate? Does Joseph think of this when he helps roll the boulder in front of the tomb where he places the dead, broken body of this man who "could have been"?

Joseph buries Jesus. What do you bet Joseph has a special place in heaven? I would be willing to wager that God pulls some strings to make sure that Joseph has such a special place because Joseph provides a place for God's boy when no one else will.

Joseph wraps Jesus in a linen cloth and places him in a really nice grave. This grave is not in the low rent section. Not everybody gets to be buried in the kind of grave that Jesus gets. Joseph is a man of means. He has earlier purchased a really nice grave plot. Why, it is a grave fit for a king. When you get to heaven, ask to see Joseph of Arimathea's place. It has to be something to behold.

The women watch. They hope somehow to go back to prepare Jesus' body for a proper burial. Really important people often get to be buried twice in this time and place. A year after the first burial, which usually takes place in a cave-like tomb, the flesh will have deteriorated enough to allow for the bones to be pulled together and buried in a small coffin-like box. This is done for important people. The women may be thinking about this as they watch. If Jesus cannot be honored in life, perhaps he can be honored in death. They hope to return and invest in Jesus' future burial.

Joseph seals the tomb with the stone. Perhaps this is one of the reasons that Pilate grants Joseph his request to take the body and bury it.

"What kind of grave are we talking about?" asks Pilate.

"It is a hewn stone cave outside the city. It will be sealed with a heavy rock, my Lord," responds Joseph.

Pilate rubs his chin and ponders the possibility of zealous disciples returning to rob the body from its resting place. A heavy stone—ah this is good.

"Yes, you can have the body. Make sure the stone is well placed."

Pilate wonders why he even cares.

Jesus is dead and buried. We say it in our churches with no change of expression. It is only a short phrase in the creed. We say it quickly so that we can get to the next phrase, "And on the third day he arose from the dead."

"Dead and buried" is only a little hill that gets in the way before we sail off the cliff and soar toward resurrection. Do not do that.

He died. It is important. He dies our death. He dies for us. God's very soul is changed this day. Joseph thinks that his "waiting expectantly for the kingdom of God" has come to a dead end when he buries Jesus. What Joseph does not know is that he just helped bring in the kingdom of God. Joseph wipes the sweat from his forehead. The work of helping to push the heavy stone to seal the entrance of the tomb is finally done.

Joseph walks away from the death having sealed not just a tomb, but a promise. He knows not what he does, but if he stops and listens to the night breeze he might just hear the very God whose kingdom he is waiting for say, "I'll show them . . . I'll show every last one of them."

Thanks, Joseph. When you finally shut your eyes on your long journey of life, the first voice you will hear is the one of that lonely figure you have helped this black Friday. He will say, "I owe you one, Joseph."

So do we. "Dead and buried." Slow down the next time you say it. Those "dead and buried" words are for you.

Chapter Sixteen

MARK 16:1–8
THE EMPTY TOMB

For those of you who have never picked up one of those scholarly commentaries, what I am about to say may come as a shock. In this first Gospel, which is perhaps the primary Gospel, there is no body.

If we just had the original ending of Mark, Easter sermons would be much different. Most all scholars agree that the original ending of Mark is at the end of chapter 16, verse 8. The text literally ends in the middle of a sentence. I write sentences all the time that end with a preposition. After all, what are prepositions for? See there.

I like the dramatic effect of ending sentences with prepositions. My many English teachers drilled into me that no matter what I think, it is not good English to end a sentence with a preposition. It is not good Greek either, but Mark does it. In the original Greek text the sentence ends with "for."

Some scholars think that the original ending of Mark is lost. Someone simply lost the last page or the scroll got too close to the fire or something. How could all of this drama build up only to have a group of terrified women leave the empty tomb and say nothing to anyone?

Mark's original ending has the women asking a big question about the big rock that is in front of the opening of the tomb. These women witnessed the rolling up of the rock at his burial and now they wonder who they can get to help roll it back.

Maybe they think they might find a few "real men" hanging around the tomb. They could sarcastically make such a comment about real men if they catch one of the disciples doing some grave-sitting. Will they find a sorrow-filled Simon hiding behind some shrub while he attempts to get a glimpse of the grave?

Maybe young John will be found somewhere, his confused love starting to surface. James and Andrew may decide it is safe to come out of hiding. Somebody has to help these women move that stone. For them, God is dead, and so is hope. All they can do now is honor death by bringing some spices. They have to do something, for the same reason that people bring another casserole to the family of a deceased person, even though they know that the family has enough food. Death brings us to the edge of helplessness.

What the women find is no help at all. The disciples are still hiding. These weary, confused men will be of no help—not just yet. But the women will soon discover that the help they need will come from a God who is not dead. While these women are sleeping a tired sleep of grief, God not only takes care of the stone, God takes care of a whole lot more.

The women do not find a dead Jesus. The only trouble is that they do not find an alive Jesus either. In Mark's Gospel the tomb is empty, but Jesus is already "going ahead of them to Galilee." We have no appearances of Jesus until some writer who cannot stand this abrupt ending adds a few in verses 9–20.

Before you start to panic and wonder about the material for next year's Easter sermon, calm down and sit with me a moment beside this empty tomb. Scholars are still arguing over the why of this ending, but let's live with it for a moment as if this is what Mark intends.

When is the last time you had Jesus "appear" to you? When is the last time you wished that he would? We not only have the added, longer ending of Mark, but we also have the other Gospel accounts of appearances, from which the longer ending of Mark probably originated. But what if we just had this short ending of Mark?

For those of us who have never seen Jesus, this might provide some interesting material for faith. We are told to walk away from the place of death trusting that he will be out there. We do not get to see any videos. We do not get to see, much less touch, anything. We simply are asked to believe that "he is alive." Is this not the way it is?

We have been "marking" the Gospel, and now Mark leaves us with a final mark that keeps us asking questions, but invites us to believe. Ah, that is the pivotal point in Mark.

From the times we have asked, "Why does Jesus not say more, do more, offer more, about who he is?"—to this final point of "Why does

Mark not say more about the resurrected body?" We are now at a final, "Why not more?"

Maybe this is the way Mark wants it to be. He would not be writing the words we now read if he has not encountered the resurrected Lord. Many of the people to whom he is writing will never see a picture of Jesus. They will not get to hear lectures by repentant disciples who now believe he is the Messiah.

Mark's readers must simply believe his account of the words of Jesus. Mark's readers must dare believe the words of that young man sitting beside the tomb all dressed in white who says, "Listen up . . . He is out there . . . He is not dead . . . Go discover his living presence."

The women are overcome. The original language says that they are literally "out of their minds." They are supposed to go tell Peter and the rest of the disciples that he is alive and ready to start something—or restart something—big, but Mark simply says they leave, and "say nothing to anyone."

Today, we know that someone blabbed. We know from other accounts about an out-of-breath Simon being outrun by the younger John on the way to this same empty tomb. We know of a bewildered Thomas reaching out to touch fresh wounds. We know of a Mary who hears her name called by someone she believes to be a gardener only to find new life in a garden full of death.

But with Mark, we have not only an ending with a preposition; we have an ending with questions: "Will you believe? Will you remain quiet about this Jesus?"

Has Mark made his mark on you? That is the question Mark would have been asking as he closes his book. This writer, who offers us so many dramatic pauses in his narrative, now ends with the biggest dramatic pause of all. Will the reader believe and profess that Jesus Christ is Lord?

Today we have no body of Jesus to touch or see. We must ask this same question. If our answer is "Yes we do believe that he is alive and out there ahead of us," then we can step forth and do our own marking. We are the ones who will be the proof that the tomb is empty because we will be full of the life Jesus gives.

Thank you, brother Mark. Thank you for believing what perhaps even you do not get to see. You believe enough to give us the story through your eyes. You listen to others tell the stories, and you collect them, and believe them. Mark, you allow Jesus to first change your life and then you give us a story to offer us the chance to have our lives changed.

You close out your story with a question of faith and ask us if we too will remain silent. You smile as you end your story because somebody has not remained silent, or you would not have known a story to tell. You tell us your story. How shall we now tell it to others?

Go into all the world and tell the story, the old, old story of Jesus and his love, and when you do, you will leave your mark, and Mark and Jesus will smile.

Questions for Reflection
and/or Discussion

Chapter One

MARK 1:1

What does it mean to say that Jesus is *the* Son of God? How do you think this statement would have struck you if had been a Jew living in Jesus' time?

MARK 1:2–8

Have you experienced the tension between the austerity that characterizes the style of John the Baptist, and the spirituality of abundance that Jesus proclaims in the Gospel of Mark?

Do ascetic practices deepen your spirituality or encourage your pride?

What is your experience of baptism, whether of water or of the Holy Spirit? Have you encountered Christians who told you that one kind of baptism is better than the other?

MARK 1:9–11

What difference would it make to you personally if we didn't have the other Gospel accounts to fill us in about the details of Jesus' birth?

Can you imagine God saying to you "This is my beloved child; in you I am well pleased"?

MARK 1:12–13

What do you think of Jody's statement that Christians need to be more aware of the baptismal vows in which we renounce the "spiritual forces of wickedness and reject the evil powers of the world'?

What does it mean to "resist Satan"? What kind of training or interior work would help us to be more able to do this? How can you incorporate this into your daily routine?

MARK 1:14–15

What is the new thing that God wants to do in your life?

How have you responded to opportunities for repentance and new beginnings in the past?

MARK 1:16–20

What was it about Jesus that caused people to leave everything and follow him?

Do you remember feeling passionate about first deciding to follow Jesus? What reawakens your passion to follow Jesus currently?

Chapter Two

MARK 2:1–12

To what extent are the spiritual and the physical related to each other? Where do you see a connection between the spiritual and the physical in your own life?

MARK 2:13–17

What rules does the church have today about who is "in" and who is "out"? Have you ever experienced feeling in "in" or "out" of a group?

In what way does Jesus kick down doors?

MARK 2:18-28

To what extent are you overly attached to old ways of seeing and doing things? What about your congregation?

Is institutional religion a help or a hindrance to your spiritual life? What would an ideal institutional religious organization look like?

Chapter Three

MARK 3:1–6

Which religious boxes full of regulations have hemmed you in, have hemmed others in? How can you be freed from these boxes?

How do you feel when you read the Gospel stories of Jesus' healings? How do you explain the times when you don't see the healing you are hoping for?

MARK 3:7–12

How can we cooperate in God's work of healing, liberation and justice, and push against the "demons" in our own lives and in society?

How can you open yourself to Jesus' healing power in your life?

Have you ever had a preacher tell you how bad you are, or how good you are, and how did you respond to that?

MARK 3:13–19A

What are the benefits of being part of a community of faith?

MARK 3:19B–27

Do Jesus' words about "losing to find, dying to live, and forsaking all in order to have" sound crazy to you?

Does your faith ever lead you to act in ways that make others wonder if you are crazy?

MARK 3:28–35

What do you think Jesus means by the "unpardonable sin"? Is there anything we can do that is outside God's forgiveness?

What are some examples of God working through people whom we consider outside "our system"?

Chapter Four

MARK 4:1–34

Do you find yourself too busy, or too preoccupied to make time to take in God's word?

What steps could you take to become like the fertile soil in this parable?

MARK 4:35–41

Chapter Five

Do you ever feel that Jesus is sleeping through a storm that you are facing? How can you trust that God is present with you at these times?

MARK 5:1–20

Are there places of darkness in your life where you need Jesus to bring you some light and life?

Have you experienced a time when "naming the demons" brings release?

MARK 5:21–43

Who do you relate to in either of these two stories? The disciples who are trying to keep Jesus task-oriented? Jairus? The woman who touches Jesus' garment? Any of the other characters?

Chapter Six

MARK 6:1–6

Do you ever feel that you may be overly comfortable with old ways and threatened by new ways of doing things? How can you determine which of the old ways should be held onto and which need to be shrugged off?

Does Jesus ever come to you in ways or forms that are unexpected? Are the stories in the Bible about Jesus or about his teachings so familiar to you that you no longer hear them? Have you ever tried other ways of reading the Bible that may bring the Bible to life for you, such as the practice of Lectio Divina, or reading different editions?

MARK 6:7–13

Do you find yourself getting so caught up in planning programs and making elaborate plans that are more complicated than they need be, that you don't spend time getting to know Jesus?

MARK 6:14–29

Herod wants to "cut" the messages of John the Baptist because they are disturbing to him. Are there teachings in the Bible that make you feel uncomfortable and that you wish you could cut?

MARK 6:30–44

Do you find it difficult to get away to a quiet place, figuratively or literally, to spend some time in the presence of Jesus? Have you ever felt indispensable?

Do you find this story reassuring, that despite limited resources, because of love being offered, amazing things are possible? Have you ever experienced anything like this?

MARK 6:45–52

Do you prefer to focus more on the divine or the human aspects of Jesus? Which characteristics of Jesus are most meaningful to you?

Do you sometimes let the need to understand everything in the Gospels get in the way of allowing Jesus to "crawl in the boat with you"?

Chapter Seven

MARK 7:1–23

Are there any groups of people or behaviors that you have a tendency to "judge"? What would be Jesus' attitude towards these individuals? How can the church shed its reputation of being judgmental?

MARK 7:24–37

Does this passage have any bearing on how we see people from other faith traditions? Is it more important to have the kind of faith Jesus admires or to have a "membership card" in a particular tradition?

Do you have a place where you can "show up and live," where you don't have to prove you don't have *any*thing wrong with you? How can we create that environment for ourselves and others in our daily lives where we can be free to be who we truly are, without shame?

Chapter Eight

MARK 8:1–21

Are there beliefs or practices in the church, or in your own life, that would cause Jesus to "sigh deeply in his spirit" today? Are there misunderstandings or controversies that you would want Jesus to clear up?

MARK 8:2-226

Do you find this story of the man who needs continued encounters with Jesus reassuring?

MARK 8:27—9:1

What would it look like for you to "lose your life in order to save it"? What would it mean for you to make Jesus the "Lord" of your life?

Chapter Nine

MARK 9:2–13

In the transfiguration, Jesus gets a "divine soaking." Is there any way that we can experience something like this?

MARK 9:14–29

What do you make of the Bible verse: "All things are possible to him who believes"? Do you find it inspiring or frustrating?

What is the role of doubt in your faith journey? Do you see doubt as a positive or a negative thing?

If you pray, why do you pray?

MARK 9:30–50

Are you of the Jewish or Greek persuasion when you think about Jesus being delivered up?

Imagine yourself sitting on Jesus' knee. What does he say to you?

Was Jesus just living a life of helpless vulnerability, or was there something greater compelling the choices he made? What does this mean for the way we live our lives?

Chapter Ten

MARK 10:1–12

In what other areas of life can one experience the tension between high expectations and forgiveness for imperfection? Do you experience this tension in your daily life?

God has special concern for the vulnerable. How can you embody this concern of God's towards others, towards yourself?

MARK 10:13–45

Are we intentional about honoring Jesus' desire that we take children and their needs seriously? What are some specific steps we can take to advocate for children?

Are you bound to possessions in such a way that they own you rather than the other way around? Is there anything we can do as a society that will provide a more equitable sharing of the world's resources?

How can you "let go" and allow your generosity, spontaneity and courage to flourish?

What does the idea of Jesus "giving his life as a ransom" mean to you?

MARK 10:46–52

Can you think of someone in your life from outside your particular religious tradition whose "vision" in spiritual matters you appreciate?

Chapter Eleven

MARK 11:1–11

Fill in the blank on the form, "What do you want your Messiah to be?" In what ways does Jesus meet or fail to meet your expectations for who he "should" be?

MARK 11:12–26

Are there any circumstances in which you are waiting for the "right time" to come along in order to take action, when it's possible that the right time is already happening?

How do you understand the passage which talks about the power of prayer (verses 22–24)? In what way can this saying of Jesus be applied to our prayer lives? Do those who pray have the power to "move mountains"?

What do you think you need that would allow you to maintain a daily prayer habit?

Do you struggle to forgive? What keeps you from forgiving a particular person?

MARK 11:27–33

What do you think is the purpose of the question about authority put to Jesus by the council of judges? Have you ever disregarded or quibbled with an authority because its requirements do not appeal to you and you do not want to comply?

Chapter Twelve

MARK 12:1–12

What attitudes do the Pharisees hold that Mark contrasts so consistently with Jesus'? Do you hold onto any attitudes that Jesus would consider Pharisaic? Does your faith community?

MARK 12:13–17

Have you ever had to make a hard decision that was influenced by your awareness of your citizenship in the kingdom of God?

How far would you go to respond to God's claim on you as a citizen of the kingdom of heaven? Would you consider civil disobedience? If so, for what cause?

MARK 12:18–27

Can you handle the fact that some things we would like to understand may have to remain a mystery for now?

Have you been on the giving or the receiving end of misappropriated scripture that has been destructive rather than life-giving? How have you responded to this? How can we make sure our application of scripture is helpful and appropriate?

MARK 12:28–37

Do you approach scripture with an open mind, or do you think you already know what it is going to say? Are you threatened or excited by the idea of exploring different ways to understand scripture? Have you experienced a time when a new understanding of some familiar scripture was rewarding or fruitful to you?

How can you root each of the directives of the Jewish "Shema" more firmly in the centrality of your being? Do you have a balanced relationship with the three "loves" or do you lean towards one of them more easily than the others?

MARK 12:38–44

How can we as individuals/communities/societies use our resources in ways that honor the many different kinds of "widows" among us whose lives are precarious?

Are you generous in your support of your faith community through your prayers, presence, gifts and service?

Chapter Thirteen

MARK 13:1–37

What would it look like to live each day as if it were your last?

What does it mean to say that the world is "in God's hands"? Do you remember a time when you expected God to "swoop down and radically change" things? What gives you comfort when you face bad news or times of difficulty and tribulation?

Chapter Fourteen

MARK 14:1–11

Are there ways in which we misunderstand or denigrate other people's devotion?

Imagine you are in the place of the woman who is pouring some of the precious ointment on Jesus' head. Hear the sound of the jar breaking and smell the strong fragrance of the nard as it runs over Jesus' hair and down his face. What is written in Jesus' expression as he meets your eyes?

MARK 14:12–25

Jesus is frustrated with people misunderstanding the nature of his power. What does Jesus try and get them to understand about his power through the medium of the last meal they shared together?

Have you had a particularly meaningful Communion/Eucharist experience that has given you insight into what Jesus is trying to demonstrate with this meal?

To what degree do you find the constant reversals that are the crux of Jesus' message and life disturbing or comforting?

MARK 14:27–42

Do you have the confidence to express your desires to God, even though you know the answers may not be what you are looking for? If God already knows what is on your heart, what is the purpose of prayer?

Have you faced a time when you know you had to go the hard way, when everything in you was screaming to go the easy way? How could you prepare yourself for future occasions when you may be faced with a similar circumstance?

Is there a sense in which we can stay awake with Jesus? Is there a sense in which we "cannot handle the truth?"

MARK 14:43–52

What do you imagine is the expression on Jesus' face when Judas reaches for his shoulders to kiss him on his cheek?

Can you relate to the "certain young man" who flees the scene?

MARK 14:53–72?

What is it about Jesus' story that has so powerfully captured people's imaginations since his time on earth?

What motivates Peter at this point in the story? How would you have counseled Peter if you had been with him during this dark time for him?

In what way is Peter's story your story?

Chapter Fifteen

MARK 15:1–20

Why is it that Jesus seems to be so passive during his exchange with Pilate and decides not to respond to the charges against him?

In what way does Jesus "become representative" to us?

MARK 15:21–41

Have you ever contemplated how it would have been for God the father during Jesus' death?

How does Jesus' despair and experience of the absence of God relate to your life experiences? Are you able to be honest with others about your despair as well as your hope?

In what sense does "Jesus scream for us"? Does it give you comfort to know that God hears your cry and that Jesus has been in that place of despair?

MARK 15:42–47

Have you ever taken much time to stop and ponder Jesus' death and burial, and how it must have been for those early followers of Jesus to watch him die after they had invested so much hope into him?

Have you ever been through a time when you felt that "God is dead" because of how he didn't live up to your expectations or hopes?

Chapter Sixteen

MARK 16:1–8

Imagine being at the scene when Mary sees the empty grave and is told that Jesus is gone ahead. What thoughts are running through your head?

What gives you confidence that the story of Jesus' resurrection from the dead is true? Have you experienced in some way his living presence?

How has Mark's Gospel made a mark on you?

Bibliography

Keck, Leander E. The New Interpreter's Bible: General Articles & Introduction, Commentary, & Reflections for Each Book of the Bible including the Apocryphal/ Deuterocanonical Books; in Twelve Volumes. Vol. 8. Nashville: Abingdon, 2007.

Lamott, Anne. Operating Instructions: a Journal of My Son's First Year. New York: Pantheon, 1993.

Lamott, Anne. Plan B: Further Thoughts on Faith. New York: Riverhead, 2005.

Mays, James Luther., and Paul J. Achtemeier. Interpretation Bible Commentary, New Testament. [Bellingham, WA]: Logos Research Systems, 1992.

Weaver, Walter P. Mark. Nashville, TN: Abingdon, 1994.

Williamson, Lamar. Mark. Atlanta, GA: J. Knox, 1983.